Tahiti
& French Polynesia
a travel survival kit

Tahiti – a travel survival kit
First edition

Published by
  Lonely Planet Publications
  PO Box 88, South Yarra, Victoria 3141, Australia
  Lonely Planet Publications
  PO Box 2001A, Berkeley, California, USA 94702

Printed by
  Colorcraft, Hong Kong

Photographs by
  Rob Kay (back cover)
  Jan Whiting (front cover)
  and Tahiti Tourist Board

First Published
  October 1985

National Library of Australia
Cataloguing in Publication Data

Kay, Rob, 1953-.
  Tahiti, a travel survival kit.

  First ed.
  Includes index.
  ISBN 0 908086 80 6

  1. Tahiti – Description and travel – 1985 – Guide-books I.
  Title.

Copyright © Rob Kay, 1985.

All rights reserved. No part of this publication may be reproduced, stored in a retrieval system or
transmitted in any form by any means, electronic, mechanical, photocopying, recording or otherwise,
except brief extracts for the purpose of review, without the written permission of the publisher and
copyright owner.

Rob Kay

Rob Kay is a 32-year-old Californian whose travel experiences are culled from having lived and worked in the destinations he writes about. He feels that only by rubbing shoulders with the local population can a travel writer even begin to transmit the true 'spirit of place'. Rob has worked as a freelance journalist in Tahiti and Fiji, a bartender and publicist in San Francisco, and a radio newsman in California's San Joaquin Valley. Rob contributes regularly to newspapers and magazines in the United States and resides in San Francisco. He is fond of balmy climates, trout fishing, and cold, dark beer.

This Edition

My first interest in French Polynesia resulted from a six month stay in 1977. During that period I had the opportunity to travel throughout the beautiful islands of French Polynesia and meet a variety of people. In a few instances, some of these acquaintances became friends for life. I returned to the islands on subsequent occasions, most recently to write this book.

For their aid and assistance I would particularly like to thank Bengt and Marie-Therese Danielsson who were unfailingly kind to someone they knew only as a vagabond and whose pioneering work in Tahiti I will always be in awe of and grateful for. I must also give thanks to the staff of OPATTI, the Tahitian government tourism office, for their aid, intelligence and generosity. Finally, I must thank UTA French Airlines for transporting me to paradise.

And the Next

Travel guides are only kept up to date by travelling. If you find errors or omissions in this book we'd very much like to hear about them. As usual the best letters will be rewarded with a free copy of the next edition, or another Lonely Planet guide if you prefer.

A Brief Explanation

To be quite accurate the title of this book need only be *French Polynesia – a travel survival kit*. But who knows where that is? It's Tahiti which is the name with the magic, so that's the name that goes on the cover. Tahiti is just one of the many islands – with evocative names like Bora Bora, Huahine, Rangiroa or Fatu Hiva – which make up the five main island groups of French Polynesia.

Dedication
To Philippe Guesdon
a loyal friend

Contents

Introduction

To this day, Tahiti, the best known of French Polynesia's 130 islands, is synonymous with the modern world's romantic vision of the South Seas. This vision is a blend of fact and fiction born from glowing reports of its earliest visitors. On his arrival in 1768, the French explorer Bougainville thought he had been transported into the Garden of Eden. He promptly named the island New Cytheria, after the birthplace of Aphrodite, the Greek goddess of love. The inhabitants' kindness was summed up in the first report of the London Missionary Society:

Their manners are affable and engaging; their step easy and firm, and graceful; their behaviour free and unguarded; always boundless in generosity towards each other, and to strangers; their tempers mild, gentle and unaffected; slow to take offense, easily pacified, and seldom retaining resentment or revenge, whatever the provocation they may have received.

Captain Wallis, the first European to set foot on Tahiti, noted that 'the women in general are very handsome, some really great beauties . . . . ' They were also very accessible, and tales of a newfound Garden of Eden filtered back to Europe.

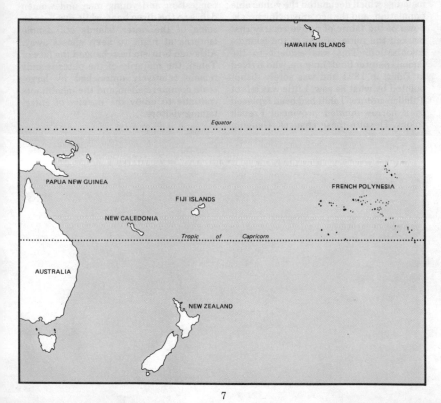

The myth of Tahiti as an unspoiled paradise was further fuelled by the 18th century philosophy of Jean-Jacques Rousseau. The reports of a nonviolent Tahitian society bound by free love coincided neatly with Rousseau's social theory that natural man was an innately good animal whose problems originated with the introduction of private property, agriculture and industry. Rousseau's adherents were elated to hear that the noble savage was alive and well in Tahiti, which proved what they had been saying all along.

Unfortunately, the tales of paradise that followed Tahiti's discovery did not match the subsequent realities of influenza, tuberculosis, venereal disease and other maladies which decimated the vulnerable population, and the accompanying breakdown of the fabric of native society that marked the initial stages of the island's colonisation. This was evident to the famous painter Paul Gauguin, who arrived in Tahiti in 1891 and was sorely disappointed by what he saw. Little was left of Tahitian culture; Tahiti had been replaced by a narrow-minded provincial French colony. Despite these changes, Gauguin immortalised the languid grace and unquenchable spirit of the Tahitian people, qualities they still possess today.

Both the advent of jet travel accompanied by tourism and the bureaucracy created by nuclear testing have accelerated change in the islands. New buildings have gone up, new jobs have been created and the cost of living has soared. Like all South Pacific island nations, French Polynesia will continue to experience the impact of 20th-century values and technology on traditional ways of life. Among the islands, Tahiti is influenced most by the west because it is a centre of tourism and trade. Meanwhile, the outer islands evolve more slowly. In Papeete, French Polynesia's capital city, residents suffer from traffic congestion and young men and women dance to the disco beat, while dwellers on some of the outer islands still kindle lanterns at night to keep ghosts away. Although tourism has changed the face of Tahiti, the majority of the outer islands remain relatively untouched by large-scale commercialism and the inhabitants continue to enjoy the novelty of entertaining visitors.

Facts about the Country

HISTORY

The most widely accepted theory of the origin of the Polynesian race is that it is a blend of peoples originating in various parts of Asia. Indications are that this amalgamation took place in the area extending from the Malay Peninsula through the islands of Indonesia. After an indeterminable period of time in this region the people made their way across the Pacific, possibly between 2000 and 1000 BC.

Perhaps the most famous alternative theory, expounded by Thor Heyerdahl, is that Polynesians may also have migrated from South America. His theory was given at least some credence by the successful crossing of the *Kon Tiki* expedition (from Peru to French Polynesia) in 1948.

Archaeologists tell us that the ancient history of Tahiti and its neighbouring islands goes back about 2000 years when the Marquesas Islands were first settled by migrations of Polynesians from Samoa. From this point of dispersal Hawaii, New Zealand, Easter Island and the Society Islands (of which Tahiti is part) were settled by ancient Polynesian mariners in huge double-hulled canoes.

The Polynesians were among the finest sailors in the world, using the sun, the stars, currents, wave motion and flight patterns of birds to navigate the vast reaches of the Pacific. When for some reason – whether tribal warfare or over-population – Polynesians had to settle elsewhere, they put their families, worldly goods, plant cuttings, animals and several months' supplies of food into their canoes and set sail to find new homes.

Through radiocarbon dating techniques and comparative studies of artifacts, scientists pinpoint the settlement of Tahiti and its neighbouring islands at around 850 AD. The most intensive research in this area is currently being undertaken by Dr Y H Sinoto of the Bishop Museum in Honolulu. In 1973 Sinoto began excavation of the Vaito'otia/Fa'ahia site (near the Bali Hai Hotel) on Huahine and found it to be the oldest settlement yet discovered in the Society Islands. Implements excavated closely match those found in the Marquesas Islands, strengthening the theory that the islands were settled by Polynesians migrating from the Marquesas.

The most visible (but certainly not the earliest) traces of pre-contact Tahitian culture are the stone remains of open-air temples called *marae*. Marae are found on all the Society Islands but nowhere are they more abundant than on Huahine. The most important marae (a national monument) is Taputaputea on Raiatea, which was the most prominent political and religious centre in the Society Islands.

First European Contact

In 1767 the English navigator Captain Samuel Wallis, commander of the *HMS Dolphin*, became the first European to set foot on Tahiti and claimed it in the name of King George III. It was pure chance that no Europeans had arrived in Tahiti earlier than Wallis. Close to 250 years had passed since Magellan sailed to the East Indies and about 20 explorers had sailed the Pacific since then. But islands were few and far between on this vast ocean and navigational aids were often inaccurate, leaving explorers with no idea where they were. Thus even if they discovered a new island, it might be difficult to ever find it again.

The initial contact between the crew of the *HMS Dolphin* and the Tahitians was of a mixed nature. The crew bartered beads, looking-glasses and knives for food and eventually for sex. Nails quickly became the most sought-after item by the Tahitians,

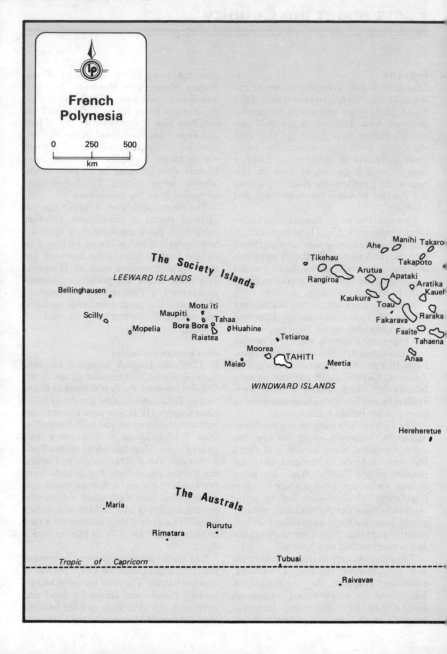

French Polynesia

0   250   500
km

Ahe   Manihi   Takaro
Tikehau   Takapoto
Arutua   Apataki
Rangiroa   Aratika
Kaukura   Kauei
Toau
Fakarava   Raraka
Faaite
Tahaena
Anaa

The Society Islands

LEEWARD ISLANDS

Bellinghausen

Scilly

Mopelia   Maupiti   Motu iti
Bora Bora   Tahaa
Raiatea   Huahine   Tetiaroa

Moorea
Maiao   TAHITI   Meetia

WINDWARD ISLANDS

Hereheretue

The Australs

Maria

Rimatara   Rurutu

Tropic   of   Capricorn   Tubuai

Raivavae

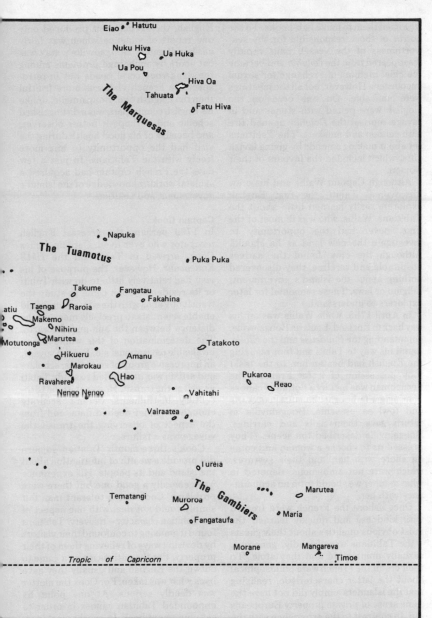

The Marquesas

Eiao   • Hatutu

Nuku Hiva

Ua Huka

Ua Pou

Hiva Oa

Tahuata

Fatu Hiva

The Tuamotus

Napuka

Puka Puka

Takume   Fangatau

Fakahina

Taenga   Raroia

atiu   Makemo

Nihiru

Marutea

Motutonga

Hikueru   Amanu

Tatakoto

Marokau

Ravahere   Hao

Pukaroa

Reao

Nengo Nengo

Vahitahi

Vairaatea

Iureia

The Gambiers

Marutea

Tematangi   Muroroa

Maria

Fangataufa

Morane   Mangareva

Timoe

Tropic of Capricorn

who used them to make fish-hooks. To the horror of those responsible for the seaworthiness of the vessel, nails rapidly disappeared from the *Dolphin* and became the chief medium of exchange for sexual encounters. However, not all the meetings were amicable. On one occasion the English were pelted with stones and in savage reprisal the *Dolphin* opened fire with cannon and muskets. The Tahitians set about making amends by giving lavish gifts, which included the favours of their women.

Although Captain Wallis and his crew 'discovered' Tahiti, the first English explorers really learned little about the Tahitians. Wallis, who was ill most of the time, never had the opportunity to investigate the new land as he should. Although the crew found the natives hospitable and carefree, they discovered nothing about the island's government, religion or laws. These remained for later explorers to understand.

In April 1768, while Wallis was on his way back to England, Louis de Bougainville, commanding the *Boudeuse* and the *Etoile*, found his way to Tahiti and (not realizing the English had beaten him to the task) took possession of it for France. The Frenchman was met by a flotilla of canoes bearing green boughs, bananas, coconuts and fowl as presents. Bougainville in return gave them nails and earrings. Bougainville described the scene: 'They pressed us to choose a woman and come on shore with her; and their gestures, which were not ambiguous, denoted in what manner we should form an acquaintance with her.'

Once ashore the French were treated with kindness and quickly learned the most obvious qualities about their guests – the Tahitians were friendly, generous, sexually uninhibited and they stole. To their credit the French were philosophical about the latter characteristic, realizing that the islanders simply did not have the same sense of private property Europeans did. In contrast to the experience with the

English, the French visit produced only one report of violence which was fairly easily mitigated. Bougainville's stay was cut short by anchorage problems among the dangerous coral heads but in retrospect the French visit was more fruitful than the English one. Bougainville, unlike his English counterpart, was a distinguished scholar and perhaps a better observer, and because of his good health during the visit had the opportunity to mix more freely with the Tahitians. In just a few days the French captain had acquired a skeletal working knowledge of the island's government and customs.

Captain Cook

In 1769 perhaps the greatest English navigator who ever lived, Captain James Cook, arrived in Tahiti on the *HMS Endeavour*. However, the purpose of his visit had relatively little to do with Tahiti or its residents. Cook came to study the transit of Venus with the sun, which would enable scientists to precisely measure the distance between the sun and the earth. The determination of this would be an invaluable navigational aid. For the voyage, an impressive group of scientists, scholars and artists was assembled to study Tahiti as well as the transit. However, their 18th-century instruments weren't accurate enough to gather needed data, and from the aspect of observing the transit the voyage was a failure.

Cook's three-month Tahitian sojourn did provide a wealth of information about the island and its people. His experience was generally a good one but there were problems. Cook was a tolerant man but simply could not deal with one aspect of the Tahitian character – thievery. Tahitians found it amusing to confound their visitors by devising ways of relieving them of their property. For the natives it was a game to outwit the English and usually they gave back what was taken. For Cook the matter was deadly serious. At one point he impounded Tahitian canoes in order to get equipment back. In another instance, he unfairly imprisoned five chiefs and held them for ransom until two of his sailors, who had deserted with their Tahitian 'wives,' were returned to his custody.

Cook cared desperately about his and his crew's behaviour towards the Tahitians and was bothered by a shooting incident that left a Tahitian dead. He was also concerned about the spread of venereal disease (which the English later blamed on the French), and about the internment of the chiefs. Two days before the *Endeavour* lifted anchor he wrote, 'We are likely to leave these people in disgust at our behaviour.' Perhaps Cook was too sensitive. One of the Tahitians' greatest qualities is their forgiving nature and when Cook left the Tahitians genuinely wept. He was to return to Tahiti two more times before his death in Hawaii.

Bligh & the Bounty

The year 1788 marked the arrival of the *HMS Bounty*, a name that will forever be associated with legendary Tahiti. It also marked the end of the era of exploration and the beginning of exploitation.

The *Bounty's* mission was to retrieve breadfruit plants needed as a cheap source of food for the numerous slaves working in West Indies plantations. Led by the infamous Captain Bligh, who has been unfairly maligned in the annals of history, the crew stayed six months in Tahiti transplanting the valuable plants into a makeshift greenhouse on the ship. They made the most of their time, befriending the very fun-loving Tahitians and living like sultans, so that some of the crew did not really wish to depart. Three weeks after leaving Tahiti a mutinous band of men led by Fletcher Christian coldly turned Bligh and 18 other men adrift in a 23-foot cutter with a minimal amount of provisions.

Bligh and his followers faced what seemed like certain death through uncharted waters, tempestuous weather and islands teeming with savage cannibals, but they miraculously travelled 5822 km

(3618 miles) and 41 days in an open craft to the Dutch-held island of Timor in Indonesia. Meanwhile, the *Bounty* returned to Tahiti searching for a safe haven. Fearing retribution, Christian left 16 doubtful mutineers on Tahiti. The remaining crew took Tahitian wives and servants on board and made several attempts to start communities on various islands, only to be chased out by angry natives. The *Bounty's* final destination was lonely Pitcairn Island, where Fletcher Christian and his men soon quarrelled. Only one survived the butchering that ensued during the following months. Christian's beloved Tahitian wife died shortly after the *Bounty* arrived on Pitcairn, and the grief-stricken Christian was shot by a Tahitian after taking up with the man's wife. The mutinous crew's descendants still live on Pitcairn Island today.

Bligh returned to Tahiti for his breadfruit – this time with a contingent of 19 Marines aboard. He was not one to take chances on another uprising. The survivors of the crew that Christian had stranded on Tahiti were rounded up by another British ship, put in shackles and taken back to England to stand trial.

Still a matter of debate is the cause of the celebrated mutiny. Historians write that the real cause of the uprising may have been the sailors' longing to return to their Tahitian girlfriends rather than Captain Bligh's cruelty. Still, subsequent novels and films (the exception being the 1983 production *Return of the Bounty* by De Laurentiis) have portrayed Bligh as a monster, when in fact the real villain may have been the unstable and perhaps emotionally disturbed Fletcher Christian. In his book *Pitcairn: Children of Mutiny*, Australian journalist Ian M Ball tells us that if anything, Bligh, a former officer under the legendary Captain Cook, was a tolerant man who treated his men better than did the average English captain of his day.

The Missionaries

As always, in the wake of explorers came the men of the cloth. In 1797, 30 members of the London Missionary Society came to Tahiti. While previous visitors had been appalled by customs such as human sacrifice, the Society seemed more distraught at the overt sexual proclivities of Tahitians. They attempted to dissuade the population from this 'immoral' behaviour by first converting the king to Christianity. Anthropologist Bengt Danielsson writes that they also persuaded the natives to drink tea, eat with a knife and fork, wear bonnets and coats, sleep in beds, sit on chairs and live in stone houses – in short, to emulate the English lower-middle-class manner of Society members. Within a few years, the missionaries succeeded in converting the entire population and managed to rid them of customs such as infanticide and human sacrifice. However, they never quite convinced the natives to give up their 'hedonistic' ways. An example of this was that even after converting to Christianity, Tahitian King Pomare II continued his relationships with two sisters (only one of whom he was married to) and died from the effects of alcoholism.

The French

In 1836 a French naval vessel under Admiral du Petit-Thours arrived in Papeete and demanded indemnity for a previous expulsion of Catholic missionaries from Tahiti. Queen Pomare, the current ruler, paid the money under threat of naval bombardment and later was forced to sign an agreement that would allow French missionaries to spread Catholicism. Admiral du Petit-Thours returned to Polynesia in 1842 and annexed the Marquesas Islands with the idea of turning them into a penal colony. In the process of procuring land, he decided to annex Tahiti as well. This move outraged the London Missionary Society and almost whipped up enough anti-French sentiment in England to send the two nations to war. The French returned to Tahiti with three ships in 1843 to take formal possession of the island. This marked the beginning of European colonisation in the South Pacific.

After the Tahitians realised the French were there to stay, they took up arms (bush knives and a few muzzle-loaders) and waged a guerrilla war on French garrisons, settlements and missionary stations that lasted three years. In the end, the Tahitians were crushed and Queen Pomare came out of hiding to become a rubber stamp monarch. Likewise, the Missionary Society, seeing the futility of resisting French influence, ceded their holdings to a French-Protestant group and headed for greener pastures.

The Islands in the 20th Century

French Polynesia remained a backwater colony until the 1960s, when three events triggered drastic changes in the islands. These were the building of an international airport in Tahiti, the beginning of nuclear weapons testing in the nearby Tuamotu Islands and the making of the MGM film *Mutiny on the Bounty* starring Marlon Brando and Trevor Howard. As tourists – lured no doubt by Hollywood's version of the islands – and military personnel flooded Tahiti in increasing numbers, the character of the once sleepy island changed dramatically. Money was pumped into the economy, new businesses sprang up to accommodate the influx of arrivals, and thousands of Polynesians left their far-flung island homes to look for work in Papeete. Suddenly, Tahiti was very much in the 20th century. The topics of the day were dissent over nuclear testing, brawls between soldiers and Tahitians, inflation and a shift from a subsistence economy to one completely based on money.

The increased French presence was not without its positive effects, such as new roads, schools, hospitals, agriculture and aquaculture projects, many new airstrips and eventually the highest standard of living in the South Pacific. Accompanying economic growth was a greater political awareness and a demand by Polynesians for more voice in the government, which was controlled more or less by France. In 1977 French Polynesia was finally granted a much greater degree of autonomy under the auspices of a new constitution. The new arrangement provided Polynesians with a larger voice in internal affairs, which included managing their own budget.

In 1984, a statute passed by the French Parliament in Paris created yet another incarnation of the French Polynesian constitution, giving Tahiti even greater self-government. For the first time the legislative body was allowed to elect its own president, Gaston Flosse, a distinguished leader of the Gaullist party. Previously the highest position a Tahitian could hold was vice president of the Territorial Assembly. Thus, instead of sharing power with the Paris-appointed High Commissioner, which as vice president he had to do, Flosse is able to run his Council of Ministers alone. The 1984 statute has not created complete autonomy for Tahiti's local government but it has increased its self-governing role tremendously. In areas that remain apart from local government control, such as defence or foreign affairs, Tahitian government has been granted the right to participate in far more negotiations regarding matters that may have a bearing on French Polynesia's future.

ECONOMY

Although French Polynesians cling to traditional values, the face of Tahiti has changed drastically in the past 25 years. The influx of money from both tourism and the large military presence has transformed the region's economy from an agriculturally based subsistence level to a modern consumer society. Money, not essential to an islander years ago, is now necessary for buying outboard motors, stereos, colour televisions, video decks, cars, motorcycles, gasoline and – when one can afford them – the latest fashions. The younger generation has become enamoured with the things money can buy

and their ability to consume is tempered only by the high price of imported goods.

The main source of hard currency for French Polynesia is the tourist industry and monies generated by bureaucracies of the metropolitan French government. The bulk of French Polynesians make their living working at jobs associated with tourism, retail business or government.

Agriculture, the second main source of revenue, plays an important role in supporting the rural population. The leading product is copra (dried coconut), produced by drying coconut meat in the sun, after which it is processed into oil for copra cakes (cattle feed), soap, cosmetics, margarine and other items. Processed coconut oil known as *monoi* is scented with flower blossoms and used locally for skin care. It makes a fine, inexpensive souvenir. Copra is a vital source of income to families on the outer islands who have difficulty eking out a living on remote islands because of poor resources and/or accessibility of distant markets. The government buys the dried coconut at higher prices to subsidise French Polynesians caught in this situation. Other aquacultural and agricultural products include cultured black pearls, pearl shell, vanilla, coffee, fruit, fish, shrimp and oysters.

Lured by the promise of a better life, French Polynesians from the outer islands have moved to Tahiti in ever greater numbers. Life in Papeete, however, is often not easy for those who have left their distant homes. In the capital the cost of living is high, and assimilation for the new inhabitants is fraught with basic problems such as finding housing and employment. In Papeete it is simply not possible to fish for an evening meal or gather fruits and vegetables from the land. Thus for those who have migrated, traditional life has been exchanged for an urban existence and all its woes. To counter this trend, the Tahitian government promotes economic development of the outer islands. Through aquaculture, tourism and commercial pearl ventures, the authorities hope to encourage the rural population to stay put.

Black Pearl Industry

Prior to the commercial exploitation of pearl shell in French Polynesia early in the 19th century, locals had utilised it for religious and decorative ornamentation as well as for implements such as fish-hooks and lures. Harvesting oysters for pearls gained importance in the Tuamotu Islands during the 1850s but it wasn't until the early 1960s that scientists began cultivation experiments with the indigenous black pearl oyster *pinctada margaritifera*. Today the pearls are cultivated in the Gambier and Tuamotu islands.

Over the last several years pearl cultivation has become an increasingly important source of income for French Polynesia, particularly as consumers become more aware of the black pearl in the international marketplace. The Tahiti Pearl Center and Museum, located on Boulevard Pomare next to the Pizzaria, was opened in May 1984 by a Tahitian entrepreneur with precisely this 'PR' factor in mind – to educate the public about the black pearl. Although the 'museum' is privately owned and is more a shop-*cum*-exhibition, it does a remarkably thorough job – through placards, display cases and videotapes – of illustrating the history of the pearl in civilisation with particular emphasis on the black pearl.

The process of 'making pearls' is briefly as follows: three to five-year-old oysters are collected by divers and selected for pearl cultivation. A nucleus, or tiny mother-of-pearl sphere fashioned from the shell of a Mississippi river mussel, is then attached to a graft of tissue from the oyster and placed inside the animal's gonad (sex organ). If all goes well, the tiny graft grows around the nucleus, an irritant which causes the slow formation of layer upon layer of black pearl. After a donor nucleus has been added to each oyster,

they are placed inside protective cages to keep them from predators. Under ideal growing conditions they are left to recuperate from the operation 18 months to three years before they are ready for harvesting. Meanwhile the shells are repeatedly inspected and hauled to the surface for cleaning. Water conditions are scrupulously checked for salinity, temperature and possible pollutants.

Only 20% of the oysters implanted with the nucleus will ever bear saleable pearls, and only 5% of the crop harvested will bear 'perfect' pearls – specimens that adhere to the exacting industry standards. Value is determined by size, lustre, sheen, colour and lack of defects such as bumps, dents or scratches. Price for a perfect pearl is about 100,000 cfp (US$625) but prices may range from 5000 cfp to 250,000 cfp (US$30 to US$1562). The museum is open from 8 am to noon and 2 to 5 pm Monday through Friday, and Saturday 8 am to noon.

GOVERNMENT

French Polynesia is governed by a 30-member territorial assembly which is elected by popular vote every five years. The members select 10 among them to form the Government Council (Conseil de Gouvernement), the most powerful ruling body. The assembly also elects the president.

French Polynesia's official status is 'Overseas Territory of France,' which roughly means it is a semi-autonomous colony, much like the United States territories of Puerto Rico and Guam. However, unlike people in the US territories, French Polynesians are permitted to vote in national elections and elect representatives (two deputies and a senator) to the metropolitan French National Assembly and Senate in Paris. Since June 1984, French Polynesia has also been represented in the European Parliament in Strasbourg.

The metropolitan French government runs French Polynesia's foreign affairs, defence, police, justice system and secondary education. In addition to local rule a French high commissioner is charged with administrative duties, especially in regards to the observance of French law. The current president of French Polynesia is Gaston Flosse, who is also a deputy in the European Parliament.

POPULATION

The population of French Polynesia is an amalgam composed roughly of 75% Polynesians, 10% Chinese and 15% Europeans. Among these racial categories exists every conceivable mixture. It would not be unusual for a Tahitian named Pierre Jamison to have ancestors of Chinese, American, Polynesian and French ancestry. Racial intermarriage, which is not frowned upon, accounts for the genetic strength and physical beauty of the inhabitants. The latest census figures (1983) list the population of French Polynesians as numbering just under 168,000, of which the vast majority live in Tahiti.

Tahitian Society

The social structure of French Polynesia is a complicated study in politics, economics and intermarriage. Economically, the Chinese are the most powerful group while the 'demis' (half-castes) control the political sphere. The demis, those of Polynesian and Caucasian blood, make up a class of Europeanised Tahitians. The demi population maintains an interesting mixture of Tahitian and European values. While some have adopted French culture and eschew speaking Tahitian, others identify with both cultures and find no shame in their Tahitian heritage. The majority of the population, those whose ancestry is mostly Polynesian, are known as *kaina* (rhymes with myna), and are at the lowest rung of the socio-economic ladder.

The Chinese first came to Tahiti as plantation workers during the time of the American Civil War. They were the labour force in a scheme hatched by two Scots businessmen to produce cotton, then unavailable in the northern United States. When the Civil War ended, the venture went bankrupt and the Chinese indentured workers remained. Through the years, Chinese have continued to migrate to Tahiti while keeping their culture. Many have married Polynesians or Europeans. Because of their wealth, they are sometimes the objects of resentment and jealousy from Polynesians, but without the Chinese to run the shops and businesses, the French Polynesian economy would be in serious trouble.

Sex & the Tahitian Myth

A visitor who is romantically inclined should be handsome and have money, preferably lots of money.
John W McDermott, travel writer

When discussing Tahiti, it is only a matter of time before the subject of sex arises. Since the time of Wallis and Cook, the myth of Tahiti as the 'Isle of Love' has flourished and is still used as a major selling point by the travel industry. As a result of books like *The Marriage of Loti* and movies such as *Mutiny On The Bounty*, countless men have travelled to Tahiti's shores in search of its beguilements.

From early accounts we learn that Tahitian women genuinely relished lovemaking. According to the accounts, sailors arrived in the islands to be greeted by boatloads of willing maidens. For Tahitians the arrival of a ship was like a circus visiting a small town. Days and nights were filled with wild abandon, rum drinking and the comic sight of pale white men in strange costume. Amorous flings had the benefit of material rewards as well, usually a trinket of some sort. In Cook's day nails were often given as gifts. This sometimes reached a hazardous stage as eager sailors began to wrench nails from the very ships themselves.

Today things are quite a bit different. Tahitians have by no means lost their gay abandon, but the male visitor is very mistaken if he thinks Tahitian women share his notions. Perhaps Tahitians are promiscuous by western standards (although after the 'sexual revolution' of the '60s this is debatable) but their behaviour shouldn't be judged according to European or American morality. The customs and traditions that rule their conduct were in existence long before white visitors appeared on the scene and are foreign to the Judeo-Christian ethic. Perhaps the biggest problem in understanding Tahitian sexuality arises from our own prurient perceptions. However, it is equally wrong to assume Tahitians are totally uninhibited and free from neuroses. As with people everywhere, they have their share of hangups and sexual problems.

A final word on the subject: for those of us lucky in love, Tahiti will be just like anywhere else, only warmer.

Tahiti's Third Sex

Homosexuality has been a culturally accepted lifestyle in Polynesia for centuries. When the Europeans came they were shocked and puzzled at the behaviour of male transvestites who did striptease acts for the crews and unabashedly had sexual relations with other men. Commenting on this behaviour, Captain Bligh said, 'It is strange that in so prolific a country as this men should be led into such sensual and beastly acts of gratification, but perhaps no place in the world are they so common or extraordinary as in this island.'

In the years that followed, the brethren from the London Missionary Society did their best to convert the Tahitians into becoming upright Protestants, but with little success. The cultural heritage of the *mahu* (transvestite) lives on and he still continues to play an important role in Polynesian culture. According to Bengt Danielsson, the mahu is 'a popular and honoured member of every village throughout the Society Islands.'

Anthropologist Robert I Levy writes that one becomes a mahu by choice, by being coaxed into the role, or both, at an early age. The individual associates primarily with females and learns to perform the traditionally feminine household tasks. After puberty, the mahu may assume a woman's role by cooking, cleaning, looking after children and wearing feminine clothing. He may dance what are normally the women's parts during festivals, often with greater skill than the women around him. In the villages he may work as a maid, and in Papeete can often find employment as a waiter, professional dancer or bartender.

Although Tahitians may poke fun at mahus there is none of the deep-seated hostility which exists towards homosexuals in the west. Young adolescents may seek out mahus for sexual favours, but generally only if there are no girls available. If a young man does have sex with a mahu, there is little stigma attached to the act. Mahus are accepted as human beings, not aberrations. In Papeete (see chapter on nightlife) there are several nightclubs which feature male striptease acts and cater to a varied sexual spectrum.

Anthropologist Danielsson fears that the mahu tradition is in danger of disappearing because of what he calls the 'brutal modernisation process.' He has already noticed the trend of mahus turning to western-style homosexual prostitution as a way of making a living in a modern society incompatible with the traditional mahu way of life.

EDUCATION

Compulsory education is mandatory in Tahiti for every child to the age of 14. Primary education begins at age five, and continues to the age of 12, when children begin secondary education.

There are several technical and vocational schools in Tahiti, and a large adult education program. Vocational training includes hotel, restaurant, nursing and teaching programs.

GEOGRAPHY

French Polynesia lies in the South Pacific halfway between Australia and California, and approximately halfway between Tokyo and Santiago. Although French Polynesia is spread over an expanse of water the size of Western Europe, the total land mass of its 130 islands adds up to only 4000 square km. The islands are divided into five archipelagos, all culturally, ethnically and climatically distinct. They include the Marquesas, the Tuamotus, the Society Islands, the Australs and the Gambiers.

Geologically, the islands are divided into two categories: atolls (or low islands) and high islands. An atoll is what Daniel Defoe had in mind when he wrote *Robinson Crusoe* – a flat island with little more than scrub growth and coconut palms. An atoll is actually a ring of coral that once surrounded a volcano. The volcano sank so all that is left is the coral, which now surrounds a lagoon. The colours of an atoll are so brilliant they assault the retina. The ocean laps at a blindingly white coral shore. The sun shines with dazzling intensity on a lagoon made up of many primitive blues and greens – lapis lazuli, cobalt and turquoise.

High islands can either be volcanic in origin or the result of an upheaval from the ocean floor, as is the phosphate island of Makatea. Their terrain can be smooth, rocky and barren or incredibly precipitous and covered with a lush rain forest. Unlike atolls, where drinking water must be collected in cisterns and limited types of crops can be grown, high islands often have an abundance of water and have the soil to support a variety of fruits and vegetables.

FORCES OF NATURE

Although many of French Polynesia's high islands are volcanic in origin, strong earthquakes are rare. Cyclones are also infrequent, but when they strike the results can be devastating. Until 1983 the Society Islands had been spared this type of natural disaster for 76 years. As a result of the warming caused by the now infamous 'El Nino,' Tahiti and neighbouring islands were battered by five consecutive cyclones in 1983 which cost one life and destroyed millions of dollars' worth of property.

If you're interested in reading about the destruction wrought by cyclones and hurricanes, locate a copy of *Islands of Desire* by Robert Dean Frisbie. The author describes in nearly unbelievable terms how, during a storm that inundated his tiny island home, he saved his family by tying them to trees.

FLORA & FAUNA

When the original settlers of French Polynesia, the Polynesians, arrived in the 7th or 8th century the variety of vegetation was limited to the seeds and spores borne by wind, sea and bird life that happened to find their way to the islands. To provide food and materials for shelter the Polynesians brought taro, yams, coconuts, bananas and breadfruit. To the bafflement of scientists they also cultivated the American sweet potato – a plant that does not exist in Asia. Later the missionaries introduced corn, cotton, sugar cane, citrus fruits, tamarinds, pineapples, guavas, figs, coffee and other vegetables. Tahiti also owes quite a bit to Edouard Raoul, a pharmacist-botanist who in 1887 brought a cargo of 1500 varieties of plants to the islands. He experimented with the cultivation of hundreds of types of fruit trees. Other tree species included kauri (from New Zealand), red cedar, eucalyptus, rubber, gum and jack. A decade after his arrival Raoul's gardens were donating about 150 species of plants to farmers to improve their stock.

In 1919 Harrison Smith, an American university professor turned botanist, purchased 340 acres in Papaeri and settled down to cultivate hundreds of plant varieties he imported from tropical regions throughout the world. Like Raoul, he, too, helped local farmers by giving them seeds and cuttings to better their crops. (For more information on Smith see the Circle Island Tour section on the Harrison W Smith Botanical Garden.)

Tahitians take pride in their gardens, which are richly ornamented with flowers and shrubs, including the frangipani and a variety of camellias. Fruits are usually abundant on every home site; during the harvest season they provide an important staple. They include a species of huge avocado, mangoes, papayas, custard apples, bananas, pomplemousse, oranges and pineapples.

Like the flora, most of the fauna found in Tahiti was introduced by humans. Pigs, dogs, chickens, lizards and even rats were brought by the Polynesians. Later, Captain Cook imported cattle and cats. The only 'wild' animals are pigs, the descendants of those that escaped domestication and now live in the bush.

RELIGION & THE SUPERNATURAL

The majority of French Polynesians are Protestants who comprise about 55% percent of the population, followed by Roman Catholics (30%), Mormons (6%), Seventh Day Adventists (2%) and a number of Buddhists and Confucianists among the Chinese colony (2%). The church is an important institution throughout the Pacific Island nations and French Polynesia is no exception. On the outer islands the local priest or minister often wields a powerful hand in community affairs. In most areas church attendance is high.

Although Christianity has spread throughout the islands, there is still a strong belief in vestiges of the pre-Christian religion. In the outlying areas especially, myths of gods, giants and supernatural creatures are spoken of as fact and it is not unusual for a person to have had encounters with *tupa'pau* (ghosts).

One man in Maupiti matter-of-factly described to me the occasion on which he had seen a dozen ghosts floating down a moonlit road outside his village. 'These ghosts,' he said, 'were the spirits of passengers who had perished in a ship-wreck several weeks earlier.' The spirits were native Maupitans returning home as the dead always do.

Accepting the locals' belief that the supernatural is a normal part of life often makes westerners question their own beliefs. In the Tuamotus, I met a young Frenchman by the name of Patrick who had spent several years living on the atoll of Ahe. He said that one evening he and an old villager were fishing in a skiff inside the atoll's lagoon. The Frenchman spotted an object resembling a ball of fire which rose from a spit of land on the lagoon's far edge and floated in the direction of the village. Awestruck by the sight, he pointed it out to the old man who sat contentedly fishing. The Tahitian glanced at the luminous ball and nonchalantly remarked that it was only the spirits returning to the village and really nothing to get excited about.

USEFUL CONCEPTS

Those who have spent any time in the Islands are sure to run into catch-phrases that are important concepts in trying to understand the Tahitian character:

Fiu – This expression encompasses varying shades of boredom, despair, hopelessness and frustration. Put yourself in the place of a person who has spent his or her life on a small island, perhaps only a bit of coral in the the midst of a blue expanse of ocean. The only stimuli are the ceaseless trade winds, the sound of the waves crashing on the reef, the sight of the sun bleaching the coral white and the sweltering heat. You can always go fishing or turn on Radio Tahiti, but this can get boring after a while. Life can be an endless monotone, and when someone mutters, 'I'm fiu' with husband or with job, very little explanation is necessary. The essence of 'fiu' is in the languorous tropical air.

Aita p'ape'a' – Another often-used expression, this translates literally as 'no problem.' It means take things the way they are and don't worry about them. It is basically the Tahitian equivalent of 'manana.' At best it implies a fatalistic and easygoing acceptance of the here and now. At worst, it is a kind of intellectual lethargy and lack of concern.

FESTIVALS

1 January *New Year's Day* – Friends and families gather for merrymaking.

January/February *Chinese New Year* – Celebrated with dances and fireworks.

April *Miss Bora Bora Contest*

May *Maire Day* – Fern exhibition in Papeete followed by a ball.

June *Miss Moorea Contest*

July *Miss Tahiti and Miss Tiurai Contest* – Miss Tahiti is chosen to represent the country in international beauty pageants. Miss Tiurai reigns over the Bastille Day celebrations.

14 July *Bastille Day* – France's Independence Day and the biggest holiday of the year. Known as *La Fete* by the French and *Tiurai* by the Polynesians, the carnival begins the week of July 14 and lasts about two weeks.

August *Night of the Guitar and Ute* – Local musicians compete in performing *ute*, satirical improvisational songs.

September *Te Vahine e te Tiare* (The Woman and the Flower) – Tahitian women dress up for floral theme ball.

1 November *All Saints Day* – Families visit cemeteries and illuminate graves with candles.

November *Thousand Flowers Contest and Pareu Day* – Exhibitions of flowers followed by (you guessed it) another ball. Attendees wear pareu dresses.

December *Tiare Tahiti* (National Flower Day) – Flowers are distributed throughout Papeete – on the streets, in hotels and on departing planes. Yet another ball.

Bastille Day

The Bastille Day celebration, or *Tiurai* as it is called in French Polynesia, is a month-long orgy of dance, food and drink. It is the islands' most important holiday, a combination of Mardi Gras, Fourth of July and Walpurgis Night rolled into one. During this period, which starts the week of 14 July and lasts until August, business grinds to a halt and is replaced by serious partying. Many island communities put on their own fete consisting of traditional dance competitions, rock 'n' roll bands, foot and canoe races, javelin throwing, spearfishing and other sports activities. The largest celebration occurs in Papeete, which assumes a carnival air. There the waterfront is turned into a fairground crowded with hastily constructed booths, makeshift bars and restaurants, ferris wheels and a grandstand for viewing the dance competition.

Tourists from all over the world and French Polynesians from throughout the islands converge on Tahiti to watch the dancing and partake in the good times. It is not unusual for Tahitians to stay up all night and party, sleep through the day, start chug-a-lugging Hinano beer and begin the cycle again. When it comes to partying, Tahitians are indefatigable; their capacity to enjoy themselves is superhuman. Tiurai is above all a time to socialise, forget your troubles, spend a good deal of money on liquor and perhaps mend fences with a neighbour.

One criticism longtime residents of Papeete have about Tiurai in their town is that it has become too commercialised. During the holiday, prices shoot up and merchants realise windfall profits. Commercialised or not, Tiurai in Papeete is packed with shoulder-to-shoulder throngs of people shoving their way along the carnival row. In one section, a crowd gathers in front of madly gesticulating Chinese shills, who spin the wheels of fortune in their gambling booths and attempt to outbark each other on bullhorns. Meanwhile, locals try their luck at the shooting galleries, vendors hawk kewpie dolls and cowboy hats, and young children tug their parents' arms in the direction of the merry-go-round. The temporary out door cafes selling beer, barbecued chicken and steak swell with inebriated tourists and Tahitians.

Outside the grandstand entrance, the scene is a mob of performers and gawkers. Troupes of tasselled, straw-skirted dancers mill around on the grass awaiting their turn to go on stage. They are the creme de la creme of all French Polynesian dancers. The troupe directors hype up the young-sters like football coaches before a big game. The air is thick with nervous energy and the scent of Tiare Tahiti blossoms. Nearly everyone has a crown of flowers on his or her head, or a single blossom behind the ear.

Tiurai offers more than a carnival atmosphere. For local entrepreneurs of the smaller island communities, the festival is economically important. Not only is it a big affair for the established merchants, but ordinary families can cash in on the holiday spirit by setting up small concessions selling food and liquor. The Tiurai festivities are in part subsidised by the French Polynesian government and the individual communities, which share the cost of maintenance and cash prizes for the various sports and competitions. The celebration also performs an important educational function. It provides French Polynesian youth with an outlet for traditional cultural expression which is more and more in danger of being lost with the encroaching influence of western culture.

LANGUAGE

The official languages of French Polynesia are Tahitian and French but other tongues spoken are Paumotu (the language of the Tuamotu Islands), Mangarevan (spoken in the Gambiers) and Marquesan (the language of the Marquesas Islands). These languages belong to the great Austronesian or Malayo-European lang-uage family. This widely scattered family includes the languages of Micronesia and Melanesia as well as Malay (the language of Malaysia and Indonesia), Malagasy (the language of Madagascar) and the original languages of Taiwan. Thus the origins of Tahitian date back 5000 years to ancient languages of Indonesia which later spread to Fiji and then to Samoa and Tonga.

The first explorers to set foot on Tahiti thought the Tahitian language childishly simple. Cook recorded 157 words and Bougainville estimated the entire vocab-ulary to be only about 500 words. Tahiti was chosen as a fertile ground for evangelical groups such as the London Missionary Society partly because Tahitian seemed a simple language to learn. As the missionaries were to discover, their assumption was certainly wrong. As each day passed they encountered subtleties that were baffling, idioms that were foreign and sounds that were confusing. The slightest change in pronunciation, barely discernible to the untrained ear, could give a very different meaning. Although there were no words to express western ideas about the arts, sciences or business there were words describing the natural environment such as the weather, the ocean, the stars, animal behaviour and the like that the Europeans could not even begin to understand – their powers of observation were not attuned to see what Tahitians took for granted.

At least one of the reasons Tahitian was so difficult for early visitors to grasp was because it was a language of oral record. People were expected to know their agenealogies and could recite them seem-ingly forever back into time. Thus they knew intimately the details of their forebears' lives and sometimes the origins of property claims. When no written language existed, memory was relied upon exclusively.

Once exclusively the language of Tahiti and its neighbours, Tahitian is now spoken on about 100 islands of French Polynesia. The language gained promin-ence because Tahiti was the most populous island and the chief one chosen for missionary work. As the written word and Christianity spread, the printed Tahitian word more or less superseded other local dialects and languages.

Like all languages, Tahitian was influenced by foreigners, mostly early missionaries and seafarers who mingled with the local population. Many languages, including Hebrew, Greek, Latin, English and French, contributed words that have become part of modern-day Tahitian. The translation of the Bible into Tahitian introduced words like *Sabati* (Sabbath); but English provided many loan words such as baby, butter, money, tea, pineapple and frying pan, which became *pepe, pata, moni, ti, painapo* and *faraipani* in Tahitian.

Pronunciation Rules
There are eight consonant sounds in Tahitian:

f	as in fried
h	as in house; pronounced 'sh' as in 'shark' when preceded by i and followed by o, as in *iho* (only, just)
m	as in man
n	as in noted
p	as in spark – shorter than the p of 'pan'
r	as in run – sometimes trilled like a Scottish r
t	as in stark – softer than the t of 'tar'
v	as in victory

Aside from the eight consonants a glottal stop is used in many words. For example, the word for 'pig' is *pua'a*; man is *ta'ata*; and coconut is *ha'ari*. An American English equivalent, as D T Tryon points out in his excellent Tahitian primer *Say It In Tahitian*, is 'co'n' for 'cotton.'

There are five vowels in Tahitian.

a	as in 'but'
e	as in 'day'
i	as in 'machine'
o	as in 'gold'
u	as in 'flute'

Although English is spoken by many shopkeepers, hotel personnel and students, it would help to speak French. If you want to talk with the people and acquire knowledge of the culture, learn Tahitian.

Names of Places

Papeete	Pa-pee-ay-tay
Raiatea	Rye-ah-tay-ah
Tahaa	Tah-ha-ah
Maupiti	Mau-pee-tee
Rangiroa	Rang-ghee-row-ah
Manihi	Mahn-nee-hee
Ahe	Ah-hay
Mangareva	Mahng-ah-rave-ah
Tubuai	Toop-oo-eye
Nuku Hiva	New-kew-hee-vah
Faaa	Fah-ah-ah
Tuamotu	Too-ah-mow-too
Huahine	Who-ah-hee-nay
Gambier	Gahm-bee-aye

Useful Words & Phrases

good morning; good day
ia ora na
your-rah-nah

good
maita'i
my-tye

very good
maita'i roa
my-tye-row-ah

no
aita
eye-tah

no good
aita maita'i
eye-tah-my-tye

no problem; don't worry
aita pe'ape'a
eye-tah-pay-ah-pay-ah

I'm bored; disgusted
fiu
phew

woman
vahine
vah-hee-nay

man
tane
tah-nay

friend
  e hoa
  ay-oh-ah
finish, finished
  oti
  woh-tee
American
  Marite
  Mah-ree-tay
goodbye
  nana
  nah-nah
thank you
  maruru
  mah-rhu-rhu
Cheers! down the hatch
  Manuia!
  Mahn-wee-ah

ancient temple
  marae
  mah-rye
house
  fare
  fah-ray
crazy
  taravana
  tar-ah-vah-nah
pretty, beautiful
  hehenehe
  hay-he-nay-he
traditional dance
  tamure
  tah-mu-ray
feast
  tama'ara'a
  tah-mah-rah

VISAS

Visitors need passports and onward tickets, but no visas are required for citizens of 41 countries – including those of North America, New Zealand and Australia – for visits of 30 days or less. Ninety-day visa-free visits are allowed citizens of the European Common Market countries. Visas can be issued without the High Commissioner's approval (in Tahiti) for stays of up to three months, or with the High Commissioner's approval for stays longer than three months. Tourist visas are issued for a maximum of six months, with a possibility of renewal for an additional six-month period. No foreigner can stay for more than a year with a tourist visa.

Entry Formalities for Yachties

Captain and crew must have valid passports and previously secured tourist visas. A five-day transit visa is also desirable. If coming from a country that has no French consulate, after five days the visitor must secure a valid visa from the Immigration Service – good for three months for all of French Polynesia, counting the first day of arrival.

Along with the visa each crew member must have a deposit in a special account at a local bank or at the Tresorerie Generale equal to the return fare from Tahiti back to the country of origin. During the yacht's stay in French Polynesia the crew list must correspond with the list of passengers made at the time of arrival. Any changes must be accounted for with the Chief of Immigration. Crew changes can only be made in harbours or anchorages where there are gendarmes. Debarkation of crew members can only be authorised if the person in question has an airline ticket with a confirmed reservation. Yachts may not stay longer than one year. A branch of the immigration office is located adjacent to the Fare Manihini (Visitors' Bureau) directly on the waterfront.

WORK PERMITS

To live and work in Tahiti is not easy for non-residents. A work permit is necessarily tied with a residence permit and is issued two months following the request for a work contract. The permit is issued in care of the employer, who is responsible for the employee's return to his or her homeland. A local is always given first priority regarding jobs so the person seeking work in Tahiti has to be able to provide a specialty not found on the island. To sum it up, landing a job in Tahiti is extremely difficult. US citizens skilled in the hotel/restaurant business may have the best chance as some of the hotels in Tahiti are owned or operated by Americans.

MONEY

US$1	= 150 cfp
A$1	= 130 cfp
£1	= 165 cfp
C$1	= 115 cfp
NZ$1	= 75 cfp
DM1	= 50 cfp

The currency used in French Polynesia is the French Pacific franc or cfp. Notes come in denominations of 100, 500, 1000 and 5000. Coins are in francs of 1, 5, 10, 20, 50 and 100. Visa credit cards are accepted (banks will give you a cash advance), as is American Express. Travellers' cheques are easily cashed. Tipping is discouraged by the management but Tahitians have been introduced to this practice and are not averse to it.

CLIMATE

French Polynesia has a climate ranging from subtropical in the southern archipelagos near the Tropic of Capricorn (Gambier and Austral) to steamy and equatorial in the Marquesas to the north. The Society and Tuamotu groups have a mild tropical climate that ranges between the two extremes. There are basically two seasons: the warm and humid period between November and April when rains can fall intermittently, and the dry season between May and October. The average annual temperature in the Society Islands is 25°C with variations from 21 to 34°C. Because of vegetation and wind factors, high islands are generally more humid than atolls, where you can enjoy the cooling influence of the trade winds.

HEALTH

Tahiti is malaria-free and inoculations are not required except for those arriving from an area infected with smallpox, cholera or yellow fever, which exempts 99.9% of visitors. Water is safe and plentiful in most areas but for the skitterish there is always bottled water, Coca Cola or Hinano beer. In some areas mosquitoes are pesky and numerous, ergo it is suggested that you bring a good insect repellent.

Listed below are guidelines and suggestions gleaned from professional medical sources regarding several major concerns in the South Pacific. When in doubt there is excellent medical care available in Tahiti and the visitor should not hesitate to see a doctor.

Sunshine

No matter how hot it feels on a given day in the tropics the sun is less filtered by the atmosphere than in other climes and is much more potent. Damage can be done to skin and eyes so take heed. To avoid horrendous sunburn use sunscreen. Tanning can still occur with sunscreen so don't be discouraged if you are not bronzed overnight. You will only peel that much sooner if you burn. A bad burn can ruin a vacation and a severe burn will require medical attention. A minor burn can be

treated with a cool shower or compresses, soothing cream or steroids. An aspirin two or three times a day will also ease the pain. Some people are allergic to ultraviolet light which results in redness, itching and pinpoint-sized blisters. For these unfortunates, clothing is the only answer. Fair-skinned people beware in the tropics!

Humidity

Humidity not only means discomfort but also the possibility of rashes caused by yeasts and fungi which thrive in the warm, moist environment. The problem is compounded by tight-fitting clothing and moist, hot skin rubbing against the same. You don't have to be a doctor to preventively deal with these difficulties. Keeping as cool and dry as possible is step number one. Loose-fitting clothing (cotton is best) is also a good idea, as are open-toed sandals. To reduce chafing, talcum powder or corn starch can be applied to body creases (under arms, on necks, under breasts, etc.) If all else fails, medications are available to combat fungal and yeast rashes.

Bacterial Infections

Besides fostering the growth of fungi and other micro-organisms the tropics are a prime breeding ground for staph bacteria. A common bacteria found on the skin, these little devils can multiply enormously under the right tropical conditions, especially if there is a cut, blister or insect bite on the skin releasing the fluids they thrive on. Infection can spread if you are not careful. To prevent this, wash the injury, no matter how insignificant, with soap and then treat it with antibiotic ointment and cover with a clean dressing.

Gastrointestinal Problems

Perhaps the most common complaint of visitors anywhere is the 'travellers' trots,' which can stem from any number of causes. There are several things you can do to guard against this. Make sure meals are cooked properly. Virtually all organisms that thrive at body temperature are killed in the cooking process. As mentioned earlier, water in French Polynesia is potable but if you have the slightest fears drink bottled water or soft drinks. Peel or thoroughly wash any fruit or vegetables purchased in a market. Peeling fruit yourself is always a good idea. Finally, avoid swimming, walking barefoot or collecting seafood from beaches or lagoons directly in front of settlements. Raw sewage is often dumped or piped into the nearest convenient grounds: the beach that forms the villagers' front yard.

For those who have never been in the South Seas, the extreme changes in humidity, food and other conditions may tax the system. The best advice is to take it easy for the first few days until you are acclimatised. Like good scouts you would do well to be prepared and bring sunscreen, Band-Aids, ice bag, baby powder/corn starch, Ace bandage, antacid, laxative, aspirin, cold tablets, cough syrup, antibiotic ointment and antihistamine.

INFORMATION

The main information office (OPATTI) is located on the quay nearly opposite the Vaima Shopping Center, in a cluster of brown buildings constructed to resemble traditional Tahitian dwellings known as fare. It is known as the Fare Manihini, which translates as 'guest house.' Inside you will likely find several 'demi' (half-caste) Tahitian women who will be more than happy to give you information in perfect English. Address of the Tahiti office is:

Fare Manihini
Boulevard Pomare
BP 65
Papeete, Tahiti
(tel 2-96-26)

Overseas addresses of the Tahiti Tourist Board are:

Australia
    BNP Building, 12 Castlereagh St, Sydney, NSW 2000 (tel (02) 213-5244)
France
    Maison de Tahiti et Ses Iles, 43 Avenue de l'Opera, Paris 75002 (tel (1) 297-4246)
Japan
    4 Fsun Building, 4-1-2 Roppongi, Minato-ku, Tokyo
USA
    2330 Westwood Boulevard, Suite 200, Los Angeles, California 90064 (tel (213) 475-2012)

In the USA the airline UTA have a toll free number (1-800-Tahiti) to call for free information on Tahiti.

CONSULATES
Austria
    BP 78, Papeete, Honorary Consul Marcel Krainer (tel 8-01-35)
Chile
    BP 952, Papeete, Immeuble Norman Hall, Rue du General De Gaulle, Honorary Consul Roger Divin (tel 3-89-19 office or 2-57-90 home)
Denmark
    BP 449, Papeete, Honorary Consul Jean Roland Devaux de Marigny (tel 2-03-09 office or 2-05-38 home)
Finland
    BP 2870, Papeete, Honorary Consul Janine Laguesse (tel 2-57-63 office or 2-97-39 home)
Italy
    BP 420, Papeete, c/o Tikichimic, Fare Ute, Papeete, Honorary Consul Augusto Confalonieri (tel 2-82-91 office or 3-9170 home)
Korea
    BP 2061, Papeete, Honorary Consul Bernard Baudry (tel 3-04-47 office or 2-58-96 office)
Monaco
    Motu Tane, Bora Bora, Honorary Consul Paul Emile Victor (tel 2-53-29)
Norway
    BP 306, Papeete, c/o Services Mobil, Fare Ute Papeete, Honorary Consul Victor Siu (tel 2-97-21 office or 2-05-62 home)
Netherlands
    BP 2804, Papeete, c/o Immeuble Wong Liao, Bdl d'Alsace, Papeete, Honorary Consul Jan Den Freejen Engelbertus (tel 2-49-37 office or 8-29-26 home)

Sweden
> BP 2, Papeete, c/o Ets Soari, Passage Cardella, Honorary Consul Michel Solari (tel 2-53-59 office or 2-47-60 home)

West Germany
> BP 452, Papeete, Rue Le Bihan-Fautaua, Honorary Consul Claude Elaine Weinmann (tel 2-99-94 office or 2-56-30 home)

BOOKS & BOOKSHOPS

A formidable number of books have been written about French Polynesia, some of them only readily available in the islands themselves. There are a number of good bookshops.

Bookshops

Hachette Pacifique on Avenue Bruat is the largest book distributor in French Polynesia and has several bookstores (known as *librairies*) in Papeete. They stock a limited number of titles in English as well as American magazines. The stores are at the following locales: Latin Quartier branch, Rue Gauguin; Le Kioske branch, Vaima Shopping Center (street level); upstairs branch, Vaima Shopping Center.

Other bookstores include *Libraire Klima*, Place Notre Dame; *Ping Pong*, next to the Moana Iti restaurant on Boulevard Pomare (sell and trade books); and *Bookstore*, across the side street from the main post office in Papeete.

Exploration & History

The classic edition of Cook's logbooks are *The Voyages of the Endeavour, 1768-1771* by Captain James Cook, edited by J C Beaglehole, four volumes (1955).

Tahiti A Paradise Lost by David Howarth (1984) is the best book I've encountered on the experience of the early explorers of French Polynesia – Wallis, Cook, Bougainville and company. It's fascinating and reads almost like a novel. A must for South Pacific addicts.

The Fatal Impact by Alan Moorehead is, along with Howarth's book, the best available historical account of early Tahiti. It centres mainly around the three voyages of Captain Cook, portraying him as a humane commander but with the premise that contact with white civilisation in general was to have horrible repercussions. Moorehead points out that within 80 years of Cook's visit to Tahiti the population decreased from 40,000 to 9000 and the culture deteriorated because of disuse; by the end of the 19th century Australia's coastal aborigines had been decimated; and 50 years after Cook's exploration of the Antarctic icepack the once plentiful whales and seals had been virtually wiped out.

Modern Accounts

Kon-Tiki by Thor Heyerdahl is a contemporary nonfiction classic describing the 1948 voyage of a crew of Europeans aboard a Polynesian-style raft sailing from the coast of South America to French Polynesia. The purpose of the voyage was to 'prove' Heyerdahl's theory that Polynesians may have migrated from the South American continent instead of Asia. Whether or not you subscribe to Heyerdahl's ideas, the book is a great adventure story.

In *Moruroa Mon Amour – The French Nuclear Tests in the Pacific* by Bengt and Marie-Therese Danielsson (1977) the Danielssons trace the history of the bomb in French Polynesia and the socioeconomic effects the programme has had in Tahiti. Danielsson, who originally came to French Polynesia aboard the *Kon-Tiki*, has been the leading spokesperson against the nuclear testing program and at times a lonely voice of conscience.

Tin Roofs & Palm Trees by Robert Trumbull (1977) is a serious socioeconomic/political overview of the South Pacific nations with a particular emphasis on their emergence into the 20th century. Trumbull is a former New York Times correspondent and writes with authority on the subject. This is a good primer on the background of the modern-day South Pacific.

Guidebooks

How to Get Lost & Found in Tahiti by John McDermott (Honolulu: Waikiki Publishing, 1979). McDermott is a retired ad man who likes to get 'lost and found' in the Pacific. His books are rambling, chatty accounts of his wanderings with his wife (the 'lady navigator'), and contain some interesting tidbits of information if you don't mind wading through a lot of verbiage.

Tahiti Circle Island Tour Guide by Bengt Danielsson (Papeete: Les Editions du Pacifique, 1981) is the most complete historical tour guide available on Tahiti or perhaps any South Pacific island for that matter. Exhaustively researched and sardonic in tone. Available only in Tahiti.

Moorea by Claude Robineau, photos by Erwin Christian (Papeete: Les Editions du Pacifique, 1983). Same format as the *Marquesas* book by the same publisher. Again, very good background information and great shots by Christian. Only in bookstores in Tahiti.

Moorea – A Complete Guide by James Siers (Wellington, New Zealand: Millwood Press, 1982). Another background book on Moorea. Whereas the above book is more concerned with history and culture, this guide reads more like a slick brochure or a travel edition of *Vogue*. Lots of practical information about shopping, where to eat, where to stay and what to do. Very nice photography, but very commercial.

Bora Bora E by Milas Hinshaw (Hollywood: Milas Hinshaw Productions, 1984). A useful guidebook and map to Bora Bora. Information on all the restaurants, historical sites, hotels, etc. Gossipy and entertaining, especially Hinshaw's unnerving experiences with *tupaupau* (spirits). Hinshaw's most memorable quote is 'E tai oe i teie puta ia ite oe i te parau mau' (Read this book and know the truth). Decide for yourself.

The Marquesas by Greg Denning, photos by Erwin Christian (Papeete: Les Editions du Pacifique, 1982). Comprehensive overview of the Marquesas with great photos by renowned Tahitian photographer, Erwin Christian. About the best book available on the Marquesas. Sold only in Tahiti.

Island Tales

The Blue of Capricorn by Eugene Burdick (1977) is a delightful collection of short stories and nonfiction essays about the South Pacific. Burdick, a master of the craft and co-author of *The Ugly American*, explores in particular the white's fascination with the tropics. One of the best collections of the South Pacific genre available.

South Seas Tales by Jack London is not London's most famous work but includes a few good tales including 'The House of Mapuhi,' the slanderous 'story' of an avaricious pearl buyer. Based on a real-life character with whom London had an axe to grind. The real-life person sued London and collected a handsome settlement.

Typee; a Real Romance of the South Seas and *Omoo: A Narrative of Adventures in the South Seas; a Sequel to Typee; or the Marquesas Islands* by Herman Melville are based on Melville's experiences in the islands.

Art & Culture

The Art of Tahiti by Terence Barrow, (Thames & Hudson, 1979) gives an overview of pre-contact Polynesian art with an emphasis on Tahiti.

Noa Noa by Paul Gauguin is an autobiographical account of Paul Gauguin in Tahiti.

Tahitians – Mind and Experience in the Society Islands by Robert I Levy (1973) is a tome-like work written by an anthropologist for anthropologist types. A bit unwieldy but packed with all kinds of cultural information. A good reference book.

TAHITI LITERATI

Ever since its depiction as a Garden of Eden by 19th-century romantics, Tahiti has attracted not only missionaries and vagabonds but artists and writers as well. The writers who have sojourned in French Polynesia read like a Who's Who of world literature. Below is a summary of their varied but always piquant experiences.

Herman Melville

In June of 1842 the *Acushnet*, a Yankee whaler, dropped anchor off Nuku Hiva in the Marquesas. Aboard the vessel, 22-year-old Herman Melville couldn't wait to step ashore. He had already faced 1½ years of deprivation at sea and knew he wouldn't be returning home until all the whale oil barrels were filled, perhaps two, three or even four years later. He and a friend named Toby stuffed a few biscuits beneath their clothing and jumped ship. They hid in the deep, forested recesses of the island's interior, safe from the ship's crew that would surely come looking for them. They hiked for days on end with little food and no shelter. The fact that Melville's leg was burning with infection made the trek even more excruciating. The two young men found their way to the Typee Valley, home of a tribe known for its ferocity.

Toby disappeared looking for medical aid for his friend and Melville was to spend the next four months with the Typees, an experience that would be the basis for his first book, *Typee*. He was treated well by the Marquesans, who gave him a servant and royal attention from Mehevi, the chief. However, Melville was never sure of the natives' intentions. Was he being treated as a distinguished visitor or simply being fattened for the kill? After all, these people were cannibals.

Fortunately for world literature, Melville survived his sojourn with the Typee, during which he was held in a sort of protective custody. He dwelt with the Marquesans neither in bliss nor in terror. He observed closely and made some startling revelations. 'There were,' said Melville, 'none of the thousand sources of irritation that the ingenuity of civilized man has created to mar his own felicity.'

He noted that there were no debtors, no orphans, no destitute, no lovesick maidens, no grumpy bachelors, no melancholy youth, no spoiled brats and none of the root of all evil – money.

Melville adapted well, enjoying the company of a vahine named Fayaway and the companionship of the men. His foot, however, was still inflamed and spiritually he was isolated. He needed medical care but the Typees were unwilling to let him go. His situation was well known on the island and with the help of sympathetic natives and a captain who was hard up for crew members, he escaped by joining up with the Sydney whaler the *Lucy Ann*, which sailed to Tahiti.

Apparently the conditions on this vessel – inedible food, cockroach and rat infestation and rotten rigging – were so god-awful that upon reaching Tahiti Melville decided to join the crew members in a mutiny rather than continue. His fellow travellers – with such romantic names as 'Doctor Long Ghost' (the ship's surgeon!), 'Bembo' (a tattooed Maori harpooner), 'Jingling Joe,' 'Long Jim,' 'Black Dan,' 'Bungs,' 'Blunt Bill' and 'Flash Jack' – didn't need much persuading. When they refused to sail and complained to British Consul Charles Wilson in Papeete, Wilson decided against the mutineers and with the support of the French Admiral Dupetit Thouars had them locked up. Melville was imprisoned in the Calabooza Beretanee, the local jail. After his release six weeks later, he went to the remote village of Tamai on Moorea (now near the airport) and talked the chief into allowing the women to dance the 'Lory-Lory' (the precursor of the Tamure), an erotic, passionate performance that the missionaries had naturally forbidden.

Four years later Melville laboriously put together *Typee: A Peep at Polynesian Life*, which received immediate attention in America and Europe. Some critics hailed it, some doubted its authenticity, and others called it 'racy.' The missionaries (who weren't treated too kindly in the book) found it appalling. Both *Typee* and *Omoo* were outspoken tirades against the ruination of the Pacific by 'civilisation.' Why, Melville asked, should the natives be forced to participate in an alien church, to kowtow to a foreign government, and to adopt strange and harmful ways of living? In *The Fatal Impact*, Alan Moorehead writes that although Melville was 'possibly libellous and certainly scandalous in much that he wrote,' his account of the 'sleaziness and inertia that had overtaken life' in Papeete in 1842 is remarkably vivid. Perhaps Melville was remarkably accurate as well. Moorehead says that many of the Tahitians – by this time caught between the missionaries, the whalers and finally the French – had 'lost the will to survive – the effort to adjust to the outside world had been too much.'

Pierre Loti

Midshipman Louis Marie Julien Viaud, who later became known to the world as Pierre Loti, first came to Tahiti in the 1880s aboard a French naval vessel. His largely autobiographical book, *The Marriage of Loti*, brought him fame and is credited with influencing Paul Gauguin to come to Tahiti. In the book he describes his friendship with Queen Pomare IV and his all consuming love affair with Rarahu, a young girl from Bora Bora.

Loti's book tells us how he came upon Rarahu bathing in a pool (which still can be visited today) in the Fautaua Valley near Papeete. There he witnessed the girl accepting a length of red ribbon from an elderly Chinese as payment for a kiss. Rarahu was poor and this type of behaviour was not unusual for a girl of little means. Nevertheless, as a result of what the incensed Frenchman saw, the Chinese in Tahiti suffered for years following the 1881 publication of *The Marriage of Loti*. Despite Loti's virulently anti-Chinese propaganda, the book did give an accurate account of life in Tahiti during the late 19th century.

Robert Louis Stevenson

Robert Louis Stevenson arrived in the Marquesas with his wife and mother in 1888, which marked the first leg of his six-year voyage to the South Seas aboard the *Casco*. The South Pacific held him spellbound and in the Marquesas the health of the nearly always frail writer improved dramatically. He spent his days wading in the lagoon, searching for shells, or on horseback. The Stevenson clan was impressed by the generosity and kindness of the locals so much that even Stevenson's mother, a staunch supporter of the missionaries, began to question whether such activities were actually beneficial to the natives.

From the Marquesas the *Casco* set sail for the Tuamotu atoll of Fakareva where the Stevensons spent the balmy evenings trading tales with Donat Rimareau, the half-caste French governor of the island. The author's *The Isle of Voices* utilised Rimareau's tales to a great degree.

Tahiti was the next stop on the *Casco's* itinerary. The travellers found Papeete to have a 'half and halfness' between western and Tahitian culture which they disliked and soon set sail for the other side of the island. There the Stevensons befriended a Tahitian princess (whom Pierre Loti had much admired) and a chief, both of whom helped them considerably. By this time Stevenson had become very ill, the family was short of money and the *Casco* needed extensive repair. The generous Tahitians, who offered the wayfarers food, shelter and moral support, were a godsend. The long stopover allowed Stevenson time to work and recuperate. Stevenson's wife wrote that the clan sailed from Tahiti for Honolulu on Christmas Day of 1888 'in a very thankful frame of mind.'

Jack London

Perhaps the most controversial American writer of his day, Jack London came to French Polynesia in 1906 on the ill-fated voyage of the *Snark*. He first arrived in the Marquesas after nearly dying of thirst at sea when one of the crew members inadvertently left the water tap open during a storm. The Londons stayed on Nuku Hiva for several weeks, renting the house used by Robert Louis Stevenson. They also visited the Typee Valley, immortalised in Melville's *Typee*, one of London's favorite childhood books. London was, however, disappointed by what he saw. Melville's vision of 19th-century French Polynesia no longer existed and London referred to the natives as 'half-breeds,' blaming the whites for the corrupting influence that decimated the Marquesan race physically and spiritually. He spent his days feasting on tropical fruits, relaxing in the sun, collecting curios and trying to ward off huge wasps and *nonos*, vicious flies that inflict a nasty bite.

Next stop was Tahiti, where London was greeted by the news that his cheques had bounced back home. To make matters worse, he did not get along with some of the French officials, and thieves stole many items from his boat. Perhaps this is why the writer did not speak of Tahiti in more flattering terms. In *The Cruise of the Snark* he wrote that 'Tahiti is one of the most beautiful spots in the world,' but that it was for the most part inhabited by 'human vermin.' He also took a dislike to a well-known pearl buyer, Emile Levy, and in *South Sea Tales* unfairly depicted the Frenchman as an avaricious businessman who cheated a native out of a huge pearl and then met a horrible death. London did not bother to change Levy's name or physical description in the story, and the pearl buyer was furious. Even the other residents of Tahiti, who were not terribly fond of the hard-driving businessman, thought London had gone too far. In the end, Levy successfully sued London, who had long since returned to the United States but paid dearly for his outpouring of venom.

Rupert Brooke

In 1915, on a hospital ship off Skyros, the great soldier/poet of the Edwardian age, Rupert Brooke, died of food poisoning at the tender age of 28.

While visiting the west coast of the United States in 1913, Brooke had suddenly decided to tour the South Seas. He came to Tahiti in January 1914 where he lingered until April, nursing an injury caused by grazing against coral. During this time he fell in love with a beautiful Tahitian, Taata (who he called 'Mamua') and composed perhaps his three best poems, 'The Great Lover,' 'Retrospect' and 'Tiare Tahiti.' According to biographer John Lehman, it was with Mamua that Brooke most likely had the only 'perfect and surely consummated love-affair of his life.' Wrote Brooke in 'Tiare Tahiti':

Mamua when our laughter ends,
And hearts and bodies, brown as white,
Are dust about the doors of friends,
Or scent a-blowing down the night,
Then, oh! then the wise agree,
Comes our immortality . . .

On returning to San Francisco Brooke's thoughts returned to Tahiti and his lover continued to haunt him. Months later, on his deathbed in the Aegean, he wrote in his last letter of instructions to a friend: 'Try to inform Taata of my death. Mlle Taata, Hotel Tiare, Papeete, Tahiti. It might find her. Give her my love.' Several years later, when Somerset Maugham came to Tahiti to research a book on Gauguin, Brooke's old friends still wept uncontrollably at the mention of his native name, 'Purpure,' the only name they knew him by.

Somerset Maugham

Among the works of the English writer Somerset Maugham is *The Moon & Sixpence*, a novel based on the life of Paul Gauguin. During WW I, when according to Maugham 'the old South Seas characters were by necessity confined to the islands,' he visited Tahiti to research the book. There he not only culled reminiscences of the painter from people who knew him but also learned more of writers like Loti, Brooke, Robert Louis Stevenson and Jack

London. Like those writers before him, Maugham was entranced by the magic of the South Seas and spent his time interviewing everyone who knew Gauguin, including businessmen, a sea captain, a hotel proprietress and others. In Maugham's words, he wanted to make the protagonist of his novel as 'credible as possible.'

Despite Maugham's enchantment with Tahiti, most of his short stories about the South Pacific – including 'Rain,' which immortalised the prostitute Sadie Thompson – took place in Samoa. Of this the author commented, 'The really significant fiction of the world today involves a husband and wife relationship, the problems that lovers encounter and overcome, a cuckolded man, a jilted woman, an unrequited or pretended love for the other. From sexual conflicts we have our revenge and homicidal motives.' However, Maugham observed that in a place like Tahiti, 'where there are sexual licenses, excesses, the condoning attitude on infidelity, a tolerance of promiscuity, and an absence of sexual possessiveness, there does not exist the emotional tension that precipitates human drama . . . . ' In addition, Maugham asserted 'that Tahiti is a French possession, and the French with their laissez-faire and menage-a-trois tolerance of sexual philanderings and indulgences don't really provide believable fictional protagonists for any human-triangle, story or play unless you want to make a comedy or farce out of the situation.'

Paul Gauguin's case, however, falls into a different category. When the artist came to Tahiti, 'the languor of this island, the Polynesian playfulness, the castrative sexuality that abounded there, could not save him from his ultimate and wretched fate. That of course was Gauguin's predetermined course of tragedy,' Maugham said.

Nordhoff & Hall

James Norman Hall and Charles Nordhoff first met in the military service at the end of WW I when they were commissioned to write a history of the Lafayette Flying Corps. They were vastly different in temperament. Hall was shy, optimistic, romantic and a native of Iowa. Nordhoff, outwardly more confident, was pessimistic, skeptical and had been raised in California. They distrusted each other at first, but their opposite natures were complementary and they eventually became the best of friends. Nordhoff convinced Hall that Tahiti was the place to go and write. When *The Atlantic* assigned them a piece on Tahiti and gave them an advance, they were on their way to the South Seas.

Years later, Tahiti had become their home and an outpouring of articles and books by the two ensued. They wrote some works separately but continued to work well as a team, and after their collaboration on a boy's adventure Nordhoff proposed doing another book in the same vein. Hall refused but instead suggested an idea that was to become the most famous seagoing novel written in the 20th century – *Mutiny On the Bounty*. During their initial research Nordhoff and Hall could scarcely believe that the most recent book on the *Bounty* incident had been published in 1831! No one had ever ventured to write a fictionalised account of the event even though it was the kind of story that begs to be transformed into literature. Based at the Aina Pare' hotel in Papeete, the two writers plunged into their work. From the British Museum they procured accounts of the voyage, the mutiny, Bligh's open-sea voyage and the bloody Pitcairn experience, along with copies of the court martial proceedings and the Admiralty blueprints of the *Bounty*. Both immersed themselves in 19th-century prose, which helped to set a common style. The resulting narrative was divided into three sections: *The Mutiny On the Bounty*, *Men Against the Sea* (Bligh's open-sea voyage) and *Pitcairn Island* (the adventures of Fletcher Christian, his mutineer cohorts and the Tahitians who accompanied them). The trilogy was completed in 1934, after five years of work. Fifty years and three cinematic versions later, the story still hasn't lost its charm and fascination.

Hall is buried facing Matavai Bay where the *Bounty* dropped anchor and where he and Nordhoff used to sit discussing their work. A bronze plaque on the grave is inscribed with a poem he wrote as a young boy:

Look to the Northward, stranger
Just over the hillside, there
Have you in your travels seen
A land more passing fair?

ART & CULTURE
Upper-class Tahitians have adopted western pop culture to a 'T'. French Polynesians wear the 'chicest' fashions, the tightest jeans, listen to the latest pop music and, if they can afford it, drive the newest American cars and Japanese motorcycles. Yet they still have their own language and customs that despite 200 years of foreign influence have not completely disappeared.

As in all cultures, modern Tahitian music and dance owe quite a bit to outside influence. The music is an admixture of popular American songs, French chansons and hymns borrowed from the missionaries. Tahitian bands equipped with the most modern Fender guitars and Yamaha amplifiers crank out endless songs about love, romance and betrayal just like any other band in the world. Traditional percussionists, who always accompany dance troupes, are one of the purest expressions of Polynesian music and are as much a part of the music scene today as electric guitarists. To hear the thunder of their drumming for the first time is a stirring experience.

Perhaps the most popularised aspect of Tahitian culture is expressed in dance, in particular the hip-shaking and often very erotic *tamure*, a step that every Tahitian is taught at an early age. The tamure resembles the Hawaiian hula from the waist down, but is more forceful, suggestive

and sometimes violent than the Hawaiian dance. Tahitian dancers have amazingly flexible and controlled hip movements – an art that has to be seen to be appreciated. The modern tamure is descended from traditional dance forms presented by troupes acting out a legend or event depicting warriors, kings, fisherfolk, heroes, priests and the like – a far cry from today's slick, often showbiz-style productions.

Cultural Renaissance
As with other Third World peoples, Tahitians experienced a cultural blossoming and reawakening in the 1970s, manifested through the 'Maohi' or 'Neo-Polynesian' artistic movement. Artists explored traditional Polynesian motifs while writers and playwrights went digging into their own mythology for themes. According to Bobby Holcomb, a respected Hawaiian-American artist who resides in Tahiti, Neo-Polynesian painters like himself utilise the Polynesian colour scale (earthy browns, reds, yellows) as well as traditional Polynesian historical and mythical themes. Neo-Polynesian art is often more abstract than traditional Pacific art and may exhibit heightened eroticism, sensuality, local flora and fauna, and classic Polynesian geometric patterns as displayed in tattoos and tapa cloth. Politically the movement produced nationalist stirrings, calling for greater autonomy or even independence from France.

Today the maelstrom has died down but the 'back to the roots' sentiment has taken hold over a greater portion of society. Teaching the Tahitian language in schools, once against the law, is now part of the curriculum. Politicians of every stripe espouse traditional Tahitian culture, and painters and artists enjoy the support of the state instead of fighting against it. In the last several years the French Polynesian government has nurtured the talents of young artists by displaying their works in exhibitions and providing cash prizes. Displays of Tahitian art and a re-enactment of ancient ceremonies – such as the crowning of a king – can be readily seen during Tiurai, the Bastille Day celebrations.

On the popular front, singers and musicians (whose profession is Tahiti's national pastime) continue to compose music for the masses on subjects they have always written about – love and the sea – while enriching their songs with reggae and Latin rhythms. Throughout the country, women's groups are reviving dying art forms such as hatmaking, mat weaving, quilting and the fashioning of floral crowns.

One of the most novel groups to appear on the cultural scene is 'Pupu Arioi,' a small but dedicated organisation that specialises in teaching children awareness of their Polynesian heritage. Named after an ancient Polynesian society that allowed members to criticise their leaders and rise in an otherwise rigid world, Pupu Arioi began its existence in 1977 as a theatre troupe. Later the group's emphasis shifted from theatre to education. Members now go from school to school, teaching teachers and pupils relaxation techniques which calm sometimes unruly children and put them into a more receptive state so as to introduce them to theatre, dance, music and costume. Children are not pushed, but nudged into thinking about their culture and traditions. Pupu Arioi members may also discuss Polynesian mythology and philosophy with the idea of educating children in the oral traditions which were once the backbone of Tahitian culture. Perhaps they will be successful in re-infusing values in a society that for many reasons has lost its old traditions.

THE MEDIA & ENTERTAINMENT

The local radio station – France Region 3, also known as Radio Tahiti – broadcasts in French and Tahitian. Along with local news and international news from the national French network, it features a pop music format with selections by French, American and Tahitian artists. The one television channel, which broadcasts in colour, carries drama, quiz shows, high-brow French programming, interviews, locally produced news and footage from international correspondents. The station also broadcasts in Tahitian and French. A new development in Tahiti broadcasting is the privately owned radio stations. These include Radio Tiare – which broadcasts in French and has mostly a pop music format – as well as two smaller district stations in Papara and Papenoo.

Newspapers & Magazines

Scattered throughout Papeete are kiosks selling the *International Herald Tribune* (flown in regularly from Paris) and the Pacific edition of *Time* as well as French, German and other European publications. Recently, *Newsweek* combined with Australia's *Bulletin* to create an interesting Austral-American hybrid, also available on news-stands.

French Polynesia is served by two daily French-language newspapers – *Les Nouvelles* and *Le Depeche de Tahiti* – and an English-language weekly, *Tahiti Sun Press*, published by American expat Al Prince. Prince covers the local scene extensively (often better than the French press) and has excellent travel trade reportage regarding hotels, airlines and tourism in general. The tabloid-style weekly is given away free at most hotels in French Polynesia.

Local general-interest magazines in French are *Tahitirama* and *Tahiti Hebdo*, both of which have TV schedules. Two English-language magazines circulating throughout the Pacific are *Pacific Islands Monthly (PIM)* and *Pacific*. PIM, published in Sydney, is an excellent regional publication and a venerable institution in the Pacific oriented mostly toward the old Anglo colonies. *Pacific*, (formerly *New Pacific*), published in Honolulu, is a younger upstart that also covers the Pacific basin but has better reportage of former US Trust Territories and current US dependencies than its rival.

Cinemas

There are seven movie houses in Papeete and a number scattered in the larger rural areas. Outside of Papeete there are even two drive-in theatres. As you would expect, most films are French, or American dubbed in French. Admission is about 500 cfp – approximately US$3.

Sports & Games

It is no understatement to call the Tahitians sports fanatics. On Tahiti there are facilities for golf, bicycle racing, tennis, basketball, track and field, soccer and swimming. French Polynesia also participates in the annual South Pacific Games, a regional Olympics-like event featuring only South Pacific athletes.

The closest thing to a national sport is *pirogue* (outrigger canoe) racing, which is highlighted during the Bastille Day celebrations of Tiurai. Tahitians take great pride in the Polynesian tradition of canoeing and were shocked in 1981 when for the first time the visiting American club, 'Imua,' trounced the leading Tahitian team in a major race. After this event, the Tahitians went to Southern California and Hawaii to race American teams and won every time.

Atimaono Golf Course

Atimaono, Tahiti's only golf course, is a 6352-metre (6950-yard) par 72. Located in the Papara district, the course area was formerly a cotton plantation established during the American Civil War to provide Europe with the fibre then in short supply. The course is a 45-minute drive from Papeete and is open daily from 8 am to 5

pm year-round. The resident pro is Exalt Hopu. Green fees are 1300 cfp for adults and 500 cfp per day. Clubs can be rented for 1500 cfp per day. Tel 7-40-32 or 7-43-41.

POST

The French Polynesian postal system is generally efficient. Because of numerous flights in and out of Papeete delivery time from the islands to the US, Australia and Europe is usually no longer than a week. The main post office in Papeete is a gleaming 20th-century wonder. Stamps from Polynesie Francaise are gorgeous and sought after by collectors. Sets are available in special philatelic windows.

Foreigners wishing to receive mail may do so by asking at the Poste Restante (general delivery) window. Holders of American Express cards and/or travellers' cheques may receive mail at the American Express office at Tahiti Tours, rue Jeanne d'Arc. Telegrams and telexes can also be sent from the post office.

TELEPHONE

Phone service in Tahiti is quite good. There are a few public phones scattered here and there but more often than not in an emergency you may have to ask a shopkeeper's permission to make a call. A local phone call costs 50-100 cfp. Long-distance or overseas calls can be made at the post office in downtown Papeete and from hotels.

GENERAL INFORMATION
Electricity

Current is 220 volts AC in the more modern hotels and 110 in the older facilities. Don't plug in a thing before you check with the hotel. If in doubt check the voltage on the light. Many hotels have converters as well for your appliances.

Security

Papeete is very safe by American big-city standards but there are still occasional reports of robberies. Some Tahitians are very poor and occasionally the youth may resort to crime. Even though this is rare, visitors are urged to keep an eye on valuables as you would anywhere else in the world. Depositing jewellery and the like in a hotel safe is a good idea. Outside Papeete and on the outer islands there are relatively few problems.

Time

French Polynesia is 10 hours behind GMT, two hours behind US Pacific Standard time and 20 hours behind Australian Eastern Standard time. Thus, when it is noon Sunday in Tahiti, it is 2 pm Sunday in Los Angeles and 8 am Monday in Sydney. Once in French Polynesia you will realise that locals have their own standard of time, usually one to two hours behind what you had planned.

Business Hours

Most businesses open their doors between 8 and 10 am and close at 5 pm. Some larger stores stay open until 7 pm; smaller family corner stores may not close until 10 pm. Banking hours are 7.45 am to 3.30 pm Monday through Friday, and some banks, ie the Bank of Tahiti, are open on Saturdays 7.45 to 11.30 am. Exchange counters are available at Faaa International Airport

PLACES TO STAY

Hotels in Papeete and in French Polynesia generally fall into two categories – expensive and very expensive. Aside from air-conditioning, beach frontage, discos, restaurants and bars, upscale resorts may provide tennis courts, swimming pools, bicycles and free snorkelling gear. Prices for this type of hotel range from US$65-125 for a single.

On the lower end of the scale is accommodation for the budget-minded traveller. These are either older hotels that lost their lustre when the more modern resorts opened up, smaller family-operated pensions, or boarding arrangements with families. These last do not afford all the luxuries but nevertheless are quite adequate for many people.

The smaller hotels may have air-conditioning, pools and lovely gardens but not much else in the way of extras. Prices range from US$25-50 for a single.

Hotel prices do not include 5% 'room tax' and – like all things in this world – are subject to change.

Camping is virtually unheard of but there are facilities on Moorea and Bora Bora.

FOOD

Four excellent varieties of food are available in Tahiti: French, Vietnamese, Chinese and Tahitian. Tahitian fare is more or less the same as in the rest of Polynesia – fish, shellfish, breadfruit, taro, cassava (manioc), pork, chicken, yams, rice and coconut. Beef, very popular in Tahiti, is rare on most of the outer islands. Vegetables such as tomatoes and

onions are grown on Tahiti and some of the outer islands, but are nonexistent on atolls. On most of the high islands, tubers such as manioc and taro are staples for the locals. Visitors soon find them bland and heavy. In the Tuamotus, where taro and manioc cannot be grown, rice, breadfruit and white bread are the main starches.

The dish most likely to be found on a French Polynesian meal table is *poisson cru*. It consists of chunks of raw fish marinated in lime juice or vinegar and salt and is usually topped with coconut cream, onions and oil. *Chevrettes*, found on most high islands, are freshwater shrimp. *Salade Russe* is a potato salad with tiny pieces of beet. Taro and manioc are usually boiled and eaten as the main starch. Taro, which is served in large slices, contains significant quantities of fluoride and keeps teeth healthy. Young taro leaves, boiled and topped with coconut cream, resemble and taste like

spinach. Finally, poi is a heavy, sweet pudding usually made with taro, bananas or papayas. It is served warm and topped with coconut milk.

The Polynesians who originally settled the islands brought with them bananas, breadfruit, taro, yams and, strangely enough, the American sweet potato. How the Polynesians got this last item is a mystery, but Dr Y H Sinoto of the Bishop Museum conjectures that Polynesian mariners made it to South America, perhaps traded with the locals and made their way back to Polynesia with the sweet potato. The missionaries later introduced sugar cane, cotton, corn, limes, oranges, guavas, pineapple, coffee and numerous other vegetables and fruits. Most Tahitians have adopted some eating habits from the French, including coffee, French bread, butter and canned goods. Unfortunately, it is a sign of the times to see them opening cans of Japanese tuna instead of fishing for the real thing.

FILM & PHOTOGRAPHY

Photographers are permitted to take 10 rolls of film when they leave the islands. Should you need them, film and photographic accessories are readily available in Papeete's modern shops but they are much more expensive than you will be accustomed to. Colour prints can be developed from Kodacolor in one hour at QSS in Papeete's Vaima Center. Agfachrome, Ektachrome 50 and Fujichrome R100 processing are also available at other locations.

Keep in mind that daylight is very intense in the tropics so if in doubt when shooting film, underexpose. That is, if you really want that photo, shoot according to what your normal meter reading dictates and then shoot another at a third to one full stop under. It's always best, of course, to take photos at dawn or dusk for best lighting conditions.

Always keep film dry and cool, and have your camera cleaned if exposed excessively to the elements – the humidity and salt air can ruin sensitive photo equipment in no time. If you plan to go through customs at airports frequently, it's advisable to buy a laminated lead pouch for film, available in any photo shop.

When taking photos of locals, smile and ask permission first. Most of the time people will be happy to let you photograph them but on other occasions some Tahitians may not want to be part of your future slide show.

THINGS TO BRING

Dress in Tahiti is almost always casual and, because of the warm climate, it is easy to subscribe to the adage 'travel light.' Unless you are planning to travel to the outer fringes of French Polynesia, say the Austral Islands, you can be certain it will always be warm, even at night. Therefore, clothing should be light. Bathing suit and shorts (both for men and women) are always practical and fashionable. Cotton shirts and dresses are also necessary, as are sandals, a windbreaker for the odd tropical downpour, a light sweater, a hat to shield you from the intense rays, sunscreen, insect repellent and perhaps small souvenirs or toys for Tahitian children.

THINGS TO BUY

Import duties imposed by the government are an important source of Tahiti's income. Despite these tariffs, Tahiti's duty-free shops offer good discounts on liquor, tobacco and perfume. For the fashion-conscious there are a number of boutiques with island-style and French clothing. Crafts, seashells and handmade shell leis sold in the market, at outdoor booths or at fairs make good mementoes. If you have money to spend, black coral and the indigenous black pearl make even nicer acquisitions. Philatelists should stop at the special booth at the post office – French Polynesia issues beautiful stamps. And if you stay long enough in the islands you will undoubtedly adopt the local article of clothing called a *pareu*. This practical item is a brightly coloured wraparound cotton cloth worn by men and women and is sold in every store.

CLOTHING

The national costume for men and women is the pareu (par-ay-you), a rectangular piece of cloth about two metres long. It can be tied a number of ways but is usually wrapped skirt-like around the waist and worn with a T-shirt. Although western men might at first cringe at the idea of wearing a skirt, they soon find that in Tahiti's often sweltering climate it is a practical item of clothing to wear around the house. Get hooked and you will find yourself bringing a few pareus back home. They come in a variety of colours and patterns and in several grades of quality.

Although flowers are ornaments rather than clothing, you will never see a race of people so enamoured with putting them in their hair. Fresh *tiare* or hibiscus blossoms are always worn behind the ear or braided with palm fronds and other greenery into floral crowns. Tradition has it that if a woman or man tucks the flower behind the left ear she or he is taken; a flower placed behind the right ear means the person is available. Tahitians joke that if someone waves a flower behind his or her head it means 'follow me.' I have never witnessed this but will report the outcome of such an invitation if fortunate enough to experience it.

SCUBA DIVING & SNORKELLING

Most of the islands of French Polynesia are bounded by reefs where tropical fish of every colour and description thrive. Snorkelling, easily learned, is safe and fascinating. Mask and fins are readily available and reasonably priced – one of the few reasonably priced items in the entire country. Fish watching is adequate

on Tahiti and Moorea but better snorkelling is found on the outer islands where marine resources have been less affected by humans.

For the serious diver there are several dive shops and outfitters who will take you out. All scuba divers must have a certificate from a doctor indicating that the individual is in good health. A medical exam can be taken in Tahiti if the diver lacks the proper papers. Divers also need a certificate indicating the depth specifications allowed. A lead diver must have an international or a French licence allowing the person full responsibility to lead divers to designated depths.

Average water temperature in lagoons is 28 to 29°C. Outside the reef, temperature ranges from 26 to 28°C.

Dive Specialists

Tahiti Aquatique, BP 6008, Faaa, Tahiti (tel 28042) is run by an American, Dick Johnson. Adjacent to the Maeva Beach Hotel, this shop operates a variety of nautical activities including glass-bottom boat trips, cruises and sailboat rentals. Johnson's guided scuba tours range from 4500 cfp (one-six people) to 2800 cfp (seven-20 people). Individual scuba lessons are 7500 cfp and underwater photography lessons 6900 cfp (choice of still or Super 8 cameras).

Tahiti Plongee, BP 2192, Papeete (tel 2-76-69) is located nine km from Papeete at the Marina Lotus and is headed by Henri Pouliquen. It is open seven days a week to divers of all levels. 'First dive' instruction available; prices start at 1700 cfp per dive.

Some of the hotels on the outer islands do have dive facilities but it is best to consult the hotels and perhaps the above experts in Tahiti before making plans.

Getting There

Apart from those people who arrive on a cruise ship or by yacht, all visitors to French Polynesia arrive by air at the Faaa Airport near Papeete, Tahiti. Air services through Tahiti are generally operated using Tahiti as an intermediate stop between Australia or New Zealand and the USA although there are also connections between Tahiti and Chile in South America via Easter Island. In fact, this flight is the only direct connection between Australasia and the South American continent. There are also some connections to other Pacific islands.

Airlines that fly to Tahiti from overseas include Air New Zealand, Lan Chile, Polynesian Airlines, Qantas, South Pacific Island Airways and UTA.

FROM THE USA

The main gateway from the United States to Tahiti is Los Angeles, and the carrier with the lion's share of passengers is UTA. Air New Zealand and Qantas also fly from the United States to Tahiti. Round-trip excursion fares from Los Angeles or San Francisco to Tahiti are US$850. From Honolulu the round trip fare is US$909. Better deals are available such as the circle Pacific fares to New Zealand (US$849) or to Australia (US$949) which can be routed via Tahiti. Alternatively discounted round trip tickets to Tahiti can be found for around US$550 from the US west coast.

FROM AUSTRALIA

There are no great discounts on direct flights to Tahiti from Australia despite the relatively short distance. The cheapest way is to make Tahiti a stop-over en route to the USA. Shop around and remember there are three pricing seasons for flights out of Australia – low, shoulder and high. The cheapest direct flight to Tahiti (low season) is a 30 day excursion fare for A$942 return – minimum eight days, maximum 30 days, no stops. (This jumps to A$1452 in the peak season). UTA flies Sydney–Tahiti return for A$1008, A$1353, A$1554 (low, shoulder, high). UTA's one-way fare is A$1132; or one-way to Los Angeles with a stop in Tahiti is A$1709. You can fly to the US west coast or Vancouver via Papeete with Qantas for A$1446 return (low season), or one-way for A$1013. Another alternative is to fly via New Zealand.

FROM NEW ZEALAND

Air New Zealand flies from Auckland to Papeete return for NZ$923 (off peak, from 1 February to 31 March); or NZ$1128 (peak, 15 November to 31 January). These fares are combinable with APEX fares from Australia, making a return flight from Melbourne to Papeete via Auckland as little as A$997. Air New Zealand fares from Melbourne to Auckland range from A$370 to A$504 return.

FROM THE UK

Few travellers are going to fly all the way to the South Pacific with a visit to Tahiti as their sole goal. Tahiti can, however, be conveniently visited en route to Australia or on a round-the-world ticket. Airline ticket discounters (bucket shops) in London offer round-the-world tickets which include Tahiti in their itinerary for £850 to £1000. Flying from London westbound to Australia it is also possible to include Tahiti – a typical example is a ticket London-New York-Los Angeles-Tahiti-Sydney for £464. As with the flights out of Asia, UTA is likely to be the operator through Tahiti although Air New Zealand flights may also be used.

FROM OTHER PACIFIC ISLANDS

There are surprisingly few connections between Tahiti and other Pacific nations.

UTA fly between Noumea in New Caledonia and Tahiti with a one-way fare of US$432. They also have a connection from Fiji, via Noumea, to Tahiti using Air Caledonie. The one-way fare is US$612. Air New Zealand fly Rarotonga to Tahiti for US$140 one-way.

There are also various circle-Pacific fares. For example Air New Zealand have a US$849 fare from Los Angeles to New Zealand with stopovers in Tahiti, Fiji or the Cook Islands. A similar ticket is available to Australia for US$949.

FROM ASIA

For several years now one of the most popular tickets out of South-East Asia to the USA has been the southern loop through the Pacific. Using UTA flights, this ticket takes you from Singapore via Jakarta-Sydney-Noumea-Auckland-Tahiti to Los Angeles. Numerous ticket discounters at Singapore, Bangkok in Thailand, or Penang in Malaysia sell tickets on this or a similar route. Typical costs are around US$800.

FROM SOUTH AMERICA

Lan Chile connects Tahiti with Santiago, Chile via Easter Island. Flying to Tahiti and then connecting with this flight is the most direct, though not the cheapest, way to fly to South America from Australia or New Zealand. The round-trip excursion fare from Papeete to Santiago is US$1319.

PACKAGE PLANS

Packages may not appeal to the vagabond but they are the way most visitors travel to the South Pacific. After you have decided what island you'd like to visit and for how long, consult an agency that specialises in Tahiti. The agent should be able to answer questions such as: Does the hotel have a mountain or oceanside view? Will your accommodation be over the water, on the beach or in the garden? Is the hotel a super deluxe one or more moderate? How far

away is the beach? A specialist will be familiar with the tour packages available and should be able to answer these questions so that there are no unhappy surprises.

A competent agent should also be able to prepare a tailor-made itinerary for the person who has special interests such as golf, snorkelling, diving, etc. In most cases US South Pacific specialists have toll-free telephone numbers and can advise you of the current air fare bargains and seasonal discounts. They should also have fares for inter-island travel. Last but not least, a reputable agency can save you money.

In the States UTA French Airlines' telephone marketing service, tel (213) 649-1810 in Los Angeles, can recommend a good agency in the US and Canada. Qantas and Air New Zealand can do the same in Australia and New Zealand. In the USA I have had exceptional service with Network Travel Planners, 202 Main Street, Venice, California 90291, tel (800) 352-8234 within California and (800) 421-9979 anywhere else in the US.

ALTERNATIVE TRANSPORT

Unfortunately, the romantic days of catching a tramp steamer in the United States and working your way across the Pacific no longer exist. Unless money is no object, the prohibitive cost of taking ships long distances makes it much more feasible to fly. However, once you are in the islands it is still possible (although difficult) to take freighters from one South Seas port to another. Booking passage on a freighter entails going down to the dock and talking the vessel's skipper into giving you a berth. If there is room aboard and the captain likes your looks, you are in luck. On US-registered ships, hitching a ride is impossible unless you have seaman's papers. The schedule of cargo vessels coming into Papeete is posted at the waterfront branch of the immigration police adjacent to the tourist office. You can also island-hop by contacting private plane owners and negotiating with them for rides.

For persons with time on their hands and adventure in their hearts, travelling to Tahiti by yacht is also feasible. To become a crew member, go to Honolulu or one of the larger ports on the western coast of the US – preferably Los Angeles, San Diego or San Francisco – which are departure points for the majority of Tahiti-bound yachts.

To find the boats headed in this direction, you must do some sleuthing down on the docks of the local yacht club. Usually notices are placed on yacht club bulletin boards by skippers needing crew members, or by potential sailors looking for a yacht. The best thing to do is ask around the docks or marine supply shops. Naturally someone who has previous sailing experience, is a gourmet chef or is a doctor will have a good chance to get on as a crew member. A six-week sailing season starts during the last half of September with a secondary 'window' opening in January and continuing through March. If you are serious about getting on a yacht, it's best to start doing research at least six months ahead of time. Get to know the people you are going to sail with and help them rig the boat. Sailing time from the US west coast to French Polynesia requires about a month, with nowhere to get off in the middle of the Pacific. Papeete is one of the major transit points for yachts in the entire South Pacific, and once you are there it is generally no problem for an experienced sailor to hitch a ride from Papeete to all points east and west.

Travelling to and within the islands of French Polynesia is not a difficult affair. Thanks to French largesse the transportation infrastructure is quite sophisticated. There are modern airstrips, well-paved highways, numerous boats and ferries, and a bus system that works. Visitors will find that most transportation is reasonably priced, and despite the general 'manana' attitude that pervades this part of the world, things generally run on time.

Since there is only one international airport in French Polynesia (Faaa near Papeete), a trip to the surrounding islands must begin on Tahiti. The two means of transport are air and copra boat. Travelling by air is the fastest and most efficient, but not necessarily the most economical. Although Air Polynesie, the local carrier, flies to quite a few destinations, it does not go to all the islands.

Copra boats, on the other hand, do go to every inhabited island, but take more time. They are, on the average, much less expensive to travel by. On shorter routes they can be a great bargain and also give you the chance to meet some of the locals who will undoubtedly be journeying with you.

A third possibility is to combine both air and sea transportation. For example, if you want to visit Ahe, which has no air service, it is possible to book a flight to nearby Manihi and then catch a speedboat from there to Ahe.

BY AIR

Since French Polynesia's importance as a military base was established in the early 1960s, the government has developed an extensive air transportation system serving all the distant archipelagos. Although it would be impractical to build runways on every island, most areas can be reached by flying to an island with an airstrip and then catching an outboard motor-powered skiff or inter-island boat to the place you wish to visit. The major carrier, Air Polynesie, provides a well-run air service to every island. For schedules go to the Air Polynesie office on Boulevard Pomare or the visitors' bureau (Fare Manihini) on the quay. Several smaller airlines also charter planes or helicopters for visitors. The chart below shows the prices in cfp for one-way flights to major destinations. There are additional flights so if you want

BILLET DE PASSAGE ET BULLETIN DE BAGAGES
PASSENGER TICKET AND BAGGAGE CHECK
TITETI MANUREVA E TITETI TAUIHA'A
Boîte Postale 314
Siège Social : PAPEETE - TAHITI
R.C. 1114
Tél : 22 333

air Polynésie

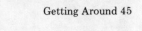

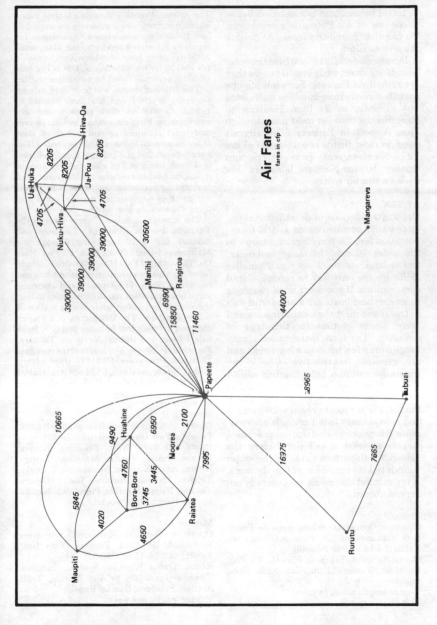

Air Fares

fares in cfp

to travel to an island not detailed below check one of Air Polynesie's brochures. To calculate round-trip fares just double the one-way fare.

In some cases flights to and from the outer islands are direct while in other cases they are routed via Papeete. For example one may fly directly from Huahine to Raiatea but in order to fly from Huahine to Rangiroa the traveller must pass through Faaa Airport in Papeete. The aircraft used on most flights is a 48-seat Fokker F27. Nineteen-seat Twin Otters and smaller Britten-Norman Islanders are used on shorter routes.

BY SEA

Despite the increase in air transportation, inter-island vessels remain a vital transportation link for travellers and cargo to the outer islands. In many instances, inter-island steamers or much smaller skiffs are the only way to reach isolated communities. If you don't mind roughing it, inter-island boats are a wonderful way to travel and meet the locals. Be sure and allow plenty of time for this type of voyaging. Trips on these vessels may range from a few hours to a few weeks and are generally inexpensive. Check the itineraries carefully before setting sail.

Boat schedules are generally reliable but like so many things in the South Pacific, are subject to change. Departure and arrival times listed are only approximate. It is recommended that one purchases tickets at least a half day before the scheduled departure date. In the outer islands tickets can be bought on the dock. Keep in mind that meals are generally not served aboard.

Aranui

Operator: Compagnie Polynesienne de Transport Maritimes, BP 220, Papeete (Motu Uta), Tahiti (tel 2-62-40 or 2-58-86)
Route: Rangiroa, Takapoto, Hiva Oa, Ua Pou, Ua Huka, Tahuata, Fatu Hiva, Nuku Hiva, Papeete
Voyage length: about 18 days

The *Aranui*, French Polynesia's largest inter-island freighter, was completely revamped in late 1984 to accommodate 40 passengers for regularly scheduled service to the Marquesas Although other inter-island boats are available (as well as air transportation), this is the only vessel specifically fitted for passenger traffic.

The 267-foot *Aranui* was built in Hamburg, Germany in 1967 and has three classes of cabins as well as deck passage and air-conditioning. First-class cabins include shower and toilet facilities; second and third class share communal showers. The only real difference between 2nd and 3rd class accommodation is a wash basin in 2nd class cabins. Accommodation has been refurbished for tourists and is large considering the boat was never designed as a passenger vessel. Bunks and three showers are provided for deck class.

The itinerary consists of three days in the Tuamotu Islands (Rangiroa, Takapoto and Arutua) and a 10-day swing through the Marquesas Islands (Nuku Hiva, Ua Pou, Hiva Oa, Tahuata and Fatu Hiva). Activities include fishing, a visit to a pearl 'farm,' land tours and horseback riding. The *Aranui* is still a working cargo boat and offers you an opportunity to visit the islands in comfort while seeing a slice of outer-island life. The ship's cook is a French chef and the daily fare includes plenty of fresh fish, lobster and shrimp. Meals are Tahitian, French and Chinese. The length of the voyage is 18 days. Prices are US$1710 (first class), US$1475 (second class), US$1404 (third class) and US$720 (deck class). Price includes three meals a day. Boats depart every 25 days.

Aura Nui II

Operator: Sunny & Bene Richmond, BP 1291, Papeete (Fare Ute), Tahiti (tel 3-76-17)
Route: Kaukura, Niau, Fakarava, Kauehi, Raraka, Katiu, Faaite, Makemo, Taenga, Nihiru, Anaa, Kaukura, Motutunga, Tuanake, Tepoto, Haraiki, Tahanea, Toau, Hikuera, Takume, Raroia, Fakahina, Puka Puka, Napuka
Voyage length: three weeks

Manava I

Operator: Heritiers Richmond, c/o Bene Richmond, BP 1291, Papeete (Fare Ute), Tahiti (tel 3-76-17 or 2-86-53)
Route: Arutua, Kaukura, Apataki, Rangiroa, Tikehau (eventually to Ahe, Manihi, Toau, Aratika, Fakarava, Raraka, Kauehi)
Voyage length: one week

Manava II
Operator: STMI (Societe des Transports Maritimes des Iles), Simeon & Pierrot Richmond, BP 1816, Papeete, Tahiti (tel 2-93-66 work, 2-74-40 or 2-69-80 home)
Route: Makatea, Rangiroa, Mataiva, Tikehau, Ahe, Manihi, Takapoto, Takaroa, Aratika, Kauehi, Fakarava, Toau, Arutua, Apataki, Kaukura
Voyage length: 15 to 17 days

Matariva
Operator: Ste Matariva, Gerant E Degage, c/o Societe des Douanes (tel 2-01-20 poste 38)
Route: Arutua, Kaukura, Apataki, Toau, Fakarava, Faaite
Voyage length: one week
Note: this ship does not take tourist passengers

Rairoa Nui
Operator: Albert Tang, BP 1187, Papeete (Avenue du Regent Paraita), Tahiti (tel 2-91-69)
Route: Tikehau Voyage length: four days, departs Monday, returns Thursday
Note: this ship does not take tourist passengers

Tereira
Operator: Karl M M Salmon & Lucien Utahia (tel 3-75-53)
Route: Kaukura, Arutua, Apataki (eventually Fakarava, Faaite)
Voyage length: one week

Taporo II
Operator: Compagnie de Navigation Inter Marquises, Jean Charles M Tekuataoa, BP 2516, Papeete (Rue Colette), Tahiti (tel 3-86-82)
Route: Hao, Amanu, Vairaatea, Tureia, Rikitea, Marutea Sud, Reao, Tatakoto, Vahitahi, Nukutavake, Hao, Amanu, Papeete (Tematangi, Anuanuraro, Hereheretue)
Voyage length: three or four weeks

Maire II
Operator: Ste Villierme & Cie, BP 1346, Papeete, Tahiti (tel 2-63-93)
Route: Moorea (Paopao)
Voyage length: one day

Tamarii Tuamotu
Operator: Mme Kong Tao Vonken & Cie, BP

2606, Papeete (Avenue du Prince Hinoi), Tahiti (tel 2-95-07)
Route: Fangatau, Napuka, Tepoto, Fakahina, Puka Puka, Tatakoto, Vahitahi, Aki Aki, Tureia, Nukutavake, Vairaatea, Amanu, Pukarua, Reao, Papeete
Voyage length: one month

Taporo IV
Operator: Compagnie Francaise Maritime de Tahiti, BP 368, Papeete (Fare Ute), Tahiti (tel 2-63-93)
Route: first voyage – Huahine, Raiatea, Bora-Bora, Tahaa, Raiatea, Huahine, Papeete – second voyage – Huahine, Raiatea, Huahine, Papeete
Voyage length: first voyage – departs Monday at about 5 pm, returns Thursday at noon – second voyage – departs Thursday at about 7 pm, returns Saturday at noon

The *Taporo IV* can carry 160 passengers, 50 in cabins, 110 on deck. Voyage times are Papeete-Huahine 11 hours, Huahine-Raiatea 2½ hours, Raiatea-Bora Bora 2 hours, Bora Bora-Tahaa 2½ hours, Tahaa-Raiatea 1 hour. Fares in cfp are:

from/to	deck	cabin
Papeete/Huahine	1000	2000
Papeete /Raiatea	1200	1680
Papeete/Bora Bora	1400	1980
Papeete/Tahaa	1200	1680
Huahine/Raiatea	800	1200
Huahine/ Tahaa	000	1000
Huahine/Bora Bora	750	1050
Raiatea/Tahaa	500	700
Raiatea/Bora Bora	800	1200
Bora Bora/Tahaa	800	1200

Temehani II
Operator: Societe de Navigation Temehani, BP 9015, Papeete (Motu Uta), Tahiti (tel 2-98-83)
Route: first voyage – Huahine, Raiatea, Bora-Bora, Tahaa, Raiatea, Huahine, Papeete – second voyage – Huahine, Raiatea, Huahine, Papeete
Voyage length: first voyage – departs Monday at about 5 pm, returns Thursday at noon – second voyage – departs Thursday at about 7 pm, returns Saturday at noon

The *Temehani II* has passenger capacity for

120 people including cabin berths for 34. Voyage times are Papeete-Huahine 11 hours, Huahine-Raiatea 2½ hours, Raiatea-Bora Bora 3½ hours, Bora Bora-Tahaa 2½ hours, Tahaa-Raiatea 1 hour. Fares in cfp are:

from/to	deck	cabin
Papeete/Huahine	1000	2000
Papeete/Raiatea	1200	2500
Papeete/Bora Bora	1400	2700
Papeete/Tahaa	1400	2700
Huahine/Raiatea	800	2000
Huahine/Tahaa	500	1000
Huahine/Bora Bora	750	1500
Raiatea/Tahaa	300	600
Raiatea/Bora Bora	800	2000
Bora Bora/Tahaa	800	2000

Tuhaa Pae II
Operator: Societe Anonyme d'Economie Mixte de Navigation des Australes, BP 1890, Papeete (Motu Uta), Tahiti (tel 2-93-67)
Route: Tubuai, Rurutu, Rimatara, Raivavae, Rapa
Voyage length: about 15 days

Vaihere
Operator: Sarl Sepna, c/o Bene Richmond, BP 1291, Papeete (Fare Ute), Tahiti (tel 3-76-17 or 2-86-53)
Route: Anaa, Marokau, Hao, Takume, Raroia, Nihiru, Taenga, Makemo, Katiu, Fakarava, Faaite, Niau, Amanu, Raraka, Kauehi, Toau (eventually Tauere, Rekareka)
Voyage length: three or four weeks

Taporo I
Operator: Societe Taporo Teaotea, BP 129, Uturoa, Raiatea (tel 6-35-52)
Route: Raiatea, Bora Bora, Maupiti, Huahine
Voyage length: six days

Saint Corentin
Operator: Lucien Utahia, Immeuble Tracqui et Fils (1er etage), Rue Leboucher, Papeete, Tahiti (tel 2-61-70 or 3-75-86)
Route: Papeete, Rangiroa, Papeete
Voyage length: four days

Passenger Vessel

An alternative to inter-island steamers when exploring the Society Islands is the 152-foot *Majestic Tahiti*, a strictly passenger vessel that debarks from Tahiti and visits Moorea, Raiatea, Bora Bora, Tahaa and Huahine.

The eight-day cruise departs from Papeete every Saturday, October through May, and offers visits to marae in Huahine, dance shows, traditional *tamara'a* (feasts), circle island tours of Bora Bora and Moorea, a trip up the Faaroa River in Raiatea and other sightseeing. Generally, no more than a single day is spent on any one island.

There are several classes of cabins (US$1699, $1589 or $1149 per person for first, second or third class) and the fare includes three meals a day.

The US-built and registered 44-cabin ship (capacity 88) was constructed in 1982 and is operated by Explorer Cruises of Seattle, Washington. For further information call (206) 625-9600 in the United States.

The newest and largest passenger vessel to ply Tahitian waters is the *SS Liberte*, a 188-metre, 23,500 ton vessel which will be based year-round in Papeete. The single-class ship, with a capacity of 715 passengers, will have seven-day cruises departing Papeete each Saturday to visit six islands including Rangiroa, Huahine, Raiatea/Tahaa, Bora Bora and Moorea. Activities include a pool, nightclub, gym, television, snorkelling, water skiing and sailing. On board will be a resident biologist, historian, anthropologist and geologist who will give cultural and natural history tours of the islands. Time is also alloted for visiting Papeete and all its diversions. The ship's operator, American-Hawaii Cruises (tel 800-227-3666), provides air supplements of US$299 roundtrip from the US west coast. Fares range from US$1195 to 1995 per person, double occupancy, for staterooms and cabins.

Copra Boats

To book passage on a copra boat, walk down to where they are moored (past the naval yard in Fare Ute in Papeete) and see what boats are in port. You can obtain a

Top: Le Truck at depot in Papeete, Tahiti (RK)
Bottom: Yachts at the quay in Papeete, Tahiti (RK)

Top: Lighter bringing passengers in from inter-island ship (TTB)
Left: Disembarking from the ferry at Huahine (RK)
Right: Horseriding on Moorea (JW)

list of all the copra boats and their destinations at the government tourist office.

Have a chat with the skippers on the dock, double check the current prices and determine where they are going, when they're departing and how long the journey takes. Often you have the option of either bringing your own food for the trip or eating the ships fare; the difference in price can be quite substantial.

Sometimes only deck passage is available, which means just that – sleeping, eating and drinking on deck with other islanders who have chosen the economy route.

Keep in mind that a round-trip voyage may last a month or more. Also, jumping ship on an island that has no air service may turn out to be a long-term commitment – it could be quite some time before another ship comes along.

A sea cruise on a copra boat can be appealing as long as things like rain, sea sickness, diesel fumes, engine noise, claustrophobia and huge cockroaches do not get on your nerves. On the other hand, the camaraderie, adventure, salt air, drifting, dreaming, guitar playing and drinking Hinano beer by moonlight are hard to beat.

BY ROAD

Except for the island of Tahiti, most areas do not have much paved highway. However, the roads that do exist are modern and well maintained. On all the islands there is a marvellous bus system consisting of owner-operators driving jitney-like vehicles known as 'Le Truck' – a triumph of small-scale, entrepreneurial capitalism. Most French Polynesians cannot afford cars or motorcycles so these buses transport the majority of the population, especially on Tahiti where commuting to work in Papeete from the 'district' has become a way of life.

On the outer islands, where commuting is not so big a factor and the population density is much smaller, buses are less frequent. On these islands (such as Bora Bora, Huahine or Moorea) it definitely behoves the visitor to rent a car, motorcycle or bicycle for the day's sightseeing rather than to depend on public transportation. Taxis can be found everywhere but tend to be expensive.

The Society Islands

The Society Islands are divided into two groups: to the east are the Windward Islands (Isles du Vent), which include Tahiti and Moorea; and to the west, the Leeward Islands (Isles sous le Vent) which comprise Raiatea, Tahaa, Huahine, Bora Bora and Maupiti.

The Society Islands were given their name by Captain James Cook, but the name originally referred only to the Leeward group. The English navigator Captain Samuel Wallis had already named Tahiti 'King George III's Island' and Moorea 'Duke of York's Island,' and Cook respected his predecessor's wishes. Later, however, both Tahiti and Moorea were included in references to the Society Islands.

But where did the name 'Society' originate? In Cook's own words, published in 1773, 'To these six islands (Raiatea, Tahaa, Huahine, Borabora, Tupai and Maupiti), as they lie contiguous to each other, I gave the names of Society Islands.' Thus the common notion that the name referred to the Royal Society or the Royal Geographical Society is false.

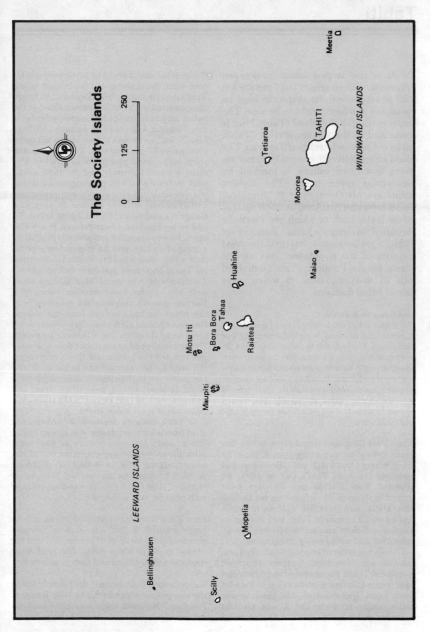

The Society Islands

LEEWARD ISLANDS

WINDWARD ISLANDS

Meetia

Tetiaroa

TAHITI

Moorea

Maiao

Huahine

Motu Iti

Tahaa

Bora Bora

Raiatea

Maupiti

Mopelia

Scilly

Bellinghausen

0   125   250

Tahiti is the largest island in French Polynesia, with an area of 1041 square km (402 square miles). Its shape can best be visualized as a figure eight on its side. The larger section of the island (Tahiti Nui) is connected to the smaller section (Tahiti Iti) by the narrow Isthmus of Taravao. The island's rugged terrain, crossed by numerous rivers and deep valleys, is marked by precipitous green peaks. The highest points are Mt Orohena at 2236 metres (7339 feet) and Mt Aorai at 2068 metres (6786 feet), both of which are eternally shrouded in wispy clouds. Because of Tahiti's mountainous interior, the vast majority of the population lives on the coastal fringes. Politically, Tahiti is divided into 20 districts, most of which were formal tribal domains.

Paul Gauguin & Tahiti

The reason why I am leaving is that I wish to live in peace and to avoid being influenced by our civilization. I only desire to create simple art. In order to achieve this, it is necessary for me to steep myself in virgin nature, to see no one but savages, to share their life and have as my sole occupation to render, just as children would do, the images of my own brain, using exclusively the means offered by primitive art, which are the only true and valid ones.

When Paul Gauguin uttered these words five weeks before his departure from France, he firmly believed that Tahiti was still an unspoiled paradise. On April Fool's Day in 1891, he departed from Europe and 69 days later arrived in Papeete. He left behind his Danish wife, Mette, and their five children in hopes that he would remain in Tahiti long enough to paint a sufficient amount of pictures for an exhibition that would establish his name.

Thanks to a letter of introduction to the local colonial administration, Gauguin was well received in Tahiti. He was wined and dined, and soon painted his first portrait in Tahiti for a fat commission. Unfortunately, the painting was unflatteringly accurate and it was his last commission for quite a while. At this point Gauguin decided it would be better to spend his time with the natives, and he moved into a Tahitian-style hut far from Papeete. Although disappointed at the little that remained of the native art and culture he had journeyed so far to see, Gauguin was happy to partake in village life. 'Koke,' as he was known to the villagers, soon took a 13-year-old wife, Teha'amana, and spent his happiest year in Tahiti with her. The artist worked feverishly and by 1893 sailed back to France with 66 paintings and a dozen wooden sculptures for his planned exhibition. Unfortunately, nobody seemed to recognise Gauguin's genius, and his exhibition failed. To add to his troubles, Mette refused to see him again, he was assaulted and severely injured by a gang of sailors, and he contracted syphilis from a Paris dance hall prostitute. He departed for Tahiti once more and on arrival sought his Tahitian wife. She would have nothing to do with him, so he found another young girl. Despite poverty and constant suffering from the injury he had received from the sailors, Gauguin finished his masterpiece, *Where do we come from? What are we? Where are we going?*. He then swallowed an enormous dose of arsenic but vomited the poison and slowly recovered. His taste for life returned and he got a job with the public works department copying building plans, fathered a child, paid off his debts and devoted much time to writing anti-government editorials in local publications.

In 1901 Gauguin received an unexpected offer from a Paris art dealer who agreed to pay him a salary for every picture he produced. With his chronic money problems out of the way, Gauguin, still in search of paradise, decided to move to the isolated Marquesan Island of Hiva Oa. Again he was disappointed with what he saw, and wrote:

Even if one is willing to pay high prices, it is no longer possible to find any of those splendid objects of bone, turtle, shell or ironwood that the natives made in olden times. The gendarmes have stolen them all and sold them to collectors.

Gauguin soon built himself the finest home in the Marquesas, which he dubbed the 'House of Pleasure.' He lived there with a 14-year-old vahine, Marie-Rose, who until then had been a resident of the Catholic mission school. With plenty of money to spend, Gauguin became well known for his wild parties and quickly incurred the wrath of the local clergy and the police. Meanwhile, his health further declined and his suffering necessitated the use of morphine. One morning a Marquesan neighbour found the artist lying on his bed with one leg hung over the edge. The visitor was not absolutely sure that his friend was still alive so he resorted to a Marquesan tradition – a bite on the head – to determine Gauguin's state. He then sang an ancient death chant.

Gauguin's legacy to modern art lies not in having introduced exotic subjects but, according to Bengt Danielsson, in having 'destroyed all existing conventions, dogmas, and academic taboos and rules that up to this time, had confined European artists to a narrow pedantic realism'. In Gauguin's own words, he provided future generations of artists with 'the right to dare anything'.

PAPEETE

The translation of Papeete is 'water (from a) basket,' which most likely means that it was a place where Tahitians came to fetch water. At the time of Cook and Wallis it was a marshland with a few scattered residents and didn't attract too much attention until 1818 when Reverend Crook of the London Missionary Society settled there with his family. Papeete began to grow in earnest when Queen Pomare made it her capital in the 1820s and sailing ships began to utilise the protected harbour, which was a much safer anchorage than Matavai Bay to the north. By the 1830s it became a regular port of call for whalers, and a number of stores, billiard halls and makeshift bars appeared on the waterfront to handle the business. When the French made Tahiti a protectorate in 1842-43 the military came on the scene, and in their footsteps came French Catholic priests and nuns.

In 1884 a fire destroyed almost half of Papeete, which resulted in an ordinance prohibiting the use of native building materials. Not much of consequence happened until 1906 when huge waves, the result of a cyclone, wiped out a number of homes and businesses. In 1914 two German men-of-war bombarded Papeete, sinking the only French naval vessel in the harbour.

Today the population of greater Papeete is over 80,000. It is French Polynesia's only real city and continues to be a major South Pacific port of call for freighters, ocean liners and yachts. Business and government revolve around the town. It is the site of the High Commissioner's residence, the Territorial Assembly, the post office, the tourist bureau, the banks, the travel agencies, movie houses, two hospitals, supermarkets, shops, hotels, nightclubs and restaurants.

Since the early 1960s Papeete has undergone a construction boom necessary to support its rising population (about 20,000 immigrants from France and 15,000 from the outer islands of French Polynesia) and modernisation. Although growth was inevitable, much of it can be attributed to the tourism infrastructure and France's nuclear testing program which resulted in an increased population growth.

Unfortunately, the growth has been at the expense of some of Papeete's beauty. Despite new apartments and offices, the town still has the provincial charm of a French colonial capital – whitewashed houses, buildings of painted wood with large verandas and corrugated tin roofs, narrow streets, parks, an outdoor market, street vendors and a profusion of odors ranging from pungent copra to the aroma of frying steaks.

Papeete is designed for walking. The sidewalks and avenues are lined with vendors selling shell necklaces, straw hats, sandwiches, sweet fried breads, pastries and candy. The aisles of the Chinese shops are crammed with cookware, rolls of brightly coloured cloth, canned goods from New Zealand and the United States, mosquito coils and imports of every variety. You get the feeling that if you poke around long enough, you might

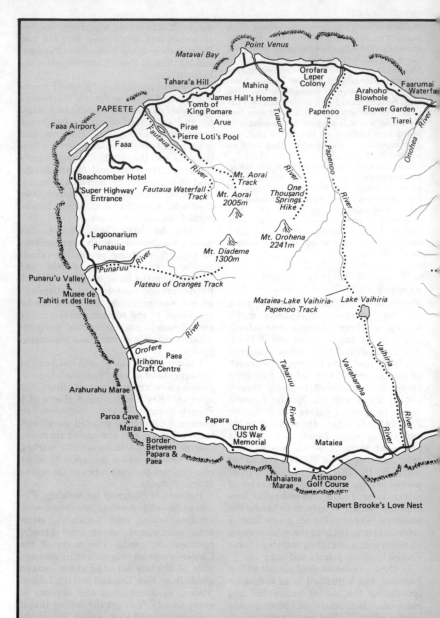

Matavai Bay
Point Venus
Orofara Leper Colony
Tahara'a Hill
Mahina
Arahoho Blowhole
Faarumai Waterfa
James Hall's Home
PAPEETE
Tomb of King Pomare
Papenoo
Flower Garden
Faaa Airport
Pirae
Arue
Tiarei
Faaa
Pierre Loti's Pool
Tuauru
Beachcomber Hotel
Mt. Aorai Track
'Super Highway' Entrance
Fautaua Waterfall Track
Mt. Aorai 2005m
One Thousand Springs Hike
Lagoonarium
Mt. Orohena 2241m
Punaauia
Mt. Diademe 1300m
Punaru'u Valley
Punaruu River
Plateau of Oranges Track
Musee de Tahiti et des Iles
Mataiea-Lake Vaihiria-Papenoo Track
Lake Vaihiria
Vaihiria River
Orofere
Paea
Irihonu Craft Centre
Taharuu River
Vairaharaha River
Arahurahu Marae
Paroa Cave
Maraa
Papara
Church & US War Memorial
Mataiea
Border Between Papara & Paea
Mahaiatea Marae
Atimaono Golf Course
Rupert Brooke's Love Nest

Fautaua River

Papenoo River

Onohea River

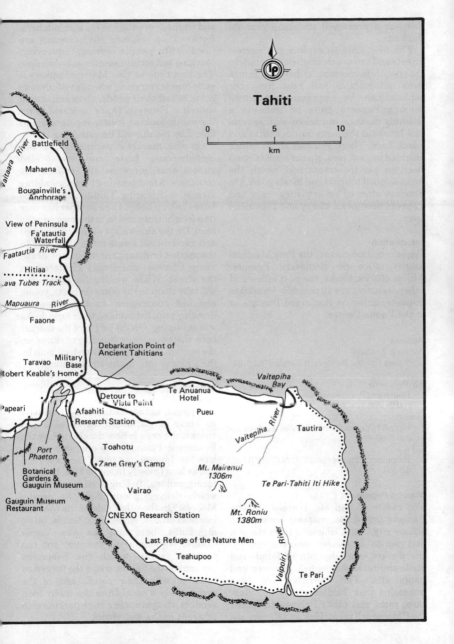

Tahiti

0   5   10
km

Vaitaara River
Battlefield
Mahaena
Bougainville's Anchorage
View of Peninsula
Fa'atautia Waterfall
Faatautia River
Hitiaa
Lava Tubes Track
Mapuaura River
Faaone

Debarkation Point of Ancient Tahitians

Taravao
Military Base
Robert Keable's Home
Papeari
Detour to Vista Point
Afaahiti Research Station
Port Phaeton
Toahotu
Zane Grey's Camp
Botanical Gardens & Gauguin Museum
Gauguin Museum Restaurant
Vairao
CNEXO Research Station
Last Refuge of the Nature Men
Teahupoo

Te Anuanua Hotel
Pueu

Vaitepiha Bay
Vaitepiha River
Tautira

Mt. Mairenui 1306m

Te Pari-Tahiti Iti Hike

Mt. Roniu 1380m

Vaipoiri River

Te Pari

discover a preserved thousand-year-old duck egg.

The best time to explore the narrow streets and browse through the stores is in the cool of the morning. Otherwise, fumes from automobiles and heat from the asphalt can be oppressive. A stroll through Papeete must be done in a leisurely manner and taken with several rest breaks at the many outdoor cafes and snack bars. There you can sit at tables shielded by canopies, sip the local Hinano beer, or eat ice cream and watch the procession of tourists and locals go by. On Sundays after 10 am activities cease and Papeete becomes a sleepy and provincial town.

Information

For information contact the Fare Manihini tourist office on Boulevard Pomare. Airline offices, banks, the post office and other resources are all centrally located in Papeete, either on Boulevard Pomare or in the Vaima Center.

Airlines

Air New Zealand
  Vaima Centre, Boulevard Pomare (tel 3-01-70)
Air Polynesie
  Boulevard Pomare (adjacent to UTA office) (tel 2-23-33)
Qantas
  Shop 54, Vaima Centre, Boulevard Pomare (tel 3-06-65)
UTA
  Boulevard Pomare (near Pitate Club) (tel 3-63-33)

Marche Papeete

The centre of Papeete, the old Marche Papeete (municipal market) covers one square city block. Shielded from the sun and rain by a massive concrete canopy, the market is a labyrinth of family-run stalls and racks selling fish, produce and handicrafts. The unwritten law here maintains that Tahitians may sell fish, taro, yams and other Polynesian foods; the Chinese sell vegetables; and Europeans

and Chinese are the bakers and butchers. Between its columns the corridors are filled with people eyeing, squeezing, touching and scrutinising the merchandise. The best time to visit Marche Papeete is early Sunday morning when out-of-towners come to sell their goods, shop and attend church in Papeete. Don't be afraid to try the exotic-looking fruits, vegetables and fish. The results will be satisfying.

On the market's perimeter are two cacophonous, fume and sweat-filled streets that serve as the town's bus terminals. Amid honking horns, rumbling diesels and blaring Tahitian music, the buses link up behind one another like cars on a freight train and inch their way up the road. On the sidewalk, swarms of barefoot and sandal-clad locals make their way to the market or disappear inside one of the many Chinese storefronts clustered on the street. While waiting for buses that will take them to the outer districts, young and old congregate on the sidewalks drinking pop, listening to their tape decks and gossiping. On the edges of the market note the two-storey buildings (stores on the bottom, living quarters on top) built by the Chinese late in the 19th century.

Waterfront

Several blocks from the market is the waterfront, known as the quay. Formerly an array of clapboard warehouses and shacks, the area is now dominated by the Boulevard Pomare. On one side of the tree-lined avenue is a row of yachts several blocks long (mostly from the US), beached racing canoes, fishing boats and ferries which deliver goods daily to nearby Moorea. On the other side of the road are business offices, storefronts, hotels, cafes, nightclubs, bars and the new Vaima Centre. Walking along the quay you can see the yachts, watch the fishermen you can see the yachts, watch the fishermen come in with their catch, and in the evening buy a meal from the many food vendors who gather in a huge parking area adjacent to the waterfront.

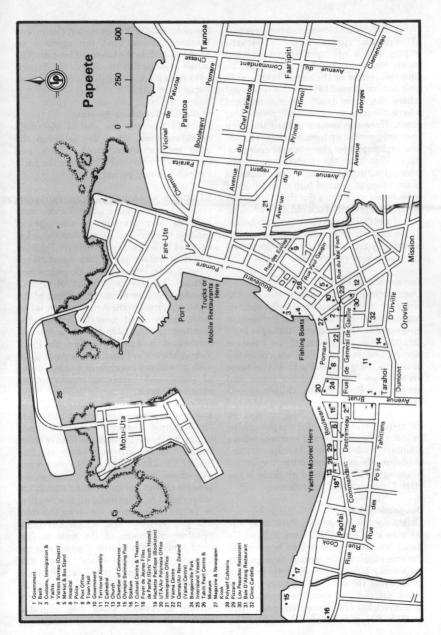

Papeete

1 Government
2 Bank
3 Customs, Immigration & Yachts
4 Visitors Bureau (Opatti)
5 Market & Bus Stand
6 Hospital
7 Police
8 Post Office
9 Town Hall
10 Government
11 Territorial Assembly
12 Cathedral
13 Church
14 Chamber of Commerce
15 Olympic Swimming Pool
16 Stadium
17 Cultural Centre & Theatre
18 Foyer de Jeunes Filles de Paofai (Girls' Youth Hostel)
19 Hachette Pacifique (Bookstore)
20 UTA/Air Polynesia Office
21 Immigration Office
22 Vaima Centre
23 Qantas/Air New Zealand (Vaima Centre)
24 Bougainville Park
25 Interisland Vessels
26 Tahiti Pearl Centre & Museum
27 Magazine & Newspaper Kiosk
28 Polyself Cafeteria
29 Pizzaria
30 Lou Pescadou Restaurant
31 Baie D'Along Restaurant
32 Clinic Cardella

When the wind blows from the direction of the docks, Papeete's air is filled with the strong aroma of copra (dried coconut meat), the main export of the islands. To find the source of the smell, take a walk past the naval yard to Fare Ute (see map) where the copra boats are moored and where there is a coconut-oil processing plant. Here the vessels unload the crop they have picked up from the outer islands and exchange it for store-bought commodities. Watching the pallets containing beer, rice, drums of kerosene, sacks of flour, cases of canned butter and jugs of wine being loaded on the rusty steamers gives you a feeling of the old days when all travel and trade were done by these boats. Try a sandwich and a bottle of Hinano at the nearby cafe where the stevedores and crew members congregate.

Territorial Assembly

Constructed in the late 1960s as the chamber of the democratically elected representatives of the French Polynesian government, this modern building is built directly over the source of the Papeete River. (The river has since been diverted to nearby Bougainville Park). In this same area Queen Pomare had her home and eventually a Royal Palace, which in typical governmental fashion was not completed until after her death. Nearby was an exclusive clubhouse for high-ranking military officers and civil servants where Gauguin (while he was still accepted) used to drink absinth. The other important building occupying these grounds is the High Commissioner's residence.

Bougainville Park

Originally named Albert Park after the Belgian king and WW I hero, this park's name was later changed to honour the French explorer. On sunny days people are usually occupying its concrete benches or enjoying the shade of its huge banyan trees. Of the two cannons prominently displayed, the one nearest the post office is off the *Seeadler*, the vessel skippered by the notorious WW I sea raider, Count Von Luckner, whose boat ran aground on Mopelia atoll in the Leeward Islands. The other belonged to the *Zelee*, the French navy boat sunk during the German raid on Papeete in 1914.

Melville's Calabooza Beretani

In 1842 this was the site of Melville's celebrated jail, where he gathered the grist for his second book, *Omoo*, and accurately described life during the early French colonial period.

BEACHES NEAR PAPEETE

One naturally associates Tahiti with beaches, and there are no shortages of sand on this tropical island. Just three km north of Papeete, near the Royal Tahitian Hotel in Pirae, is a black sand beach fringed with ironwood trees, palms and shrubs. Offshore is a beautiful view of Moorea. Further north, at the foot of the Tahara'a Hotel in the Arue district, is one more black sand beach, perhaps the loveliest on the island. Just a few km further north of the Tahara'a is the Point Venus/Museum of Discovery area, popular with picnickers because of a shady grove of palm and ironwood trees and an excellent beach.

To find a white sand beach you must go south of Papeete – about 10 to 15 km – to the 'high-rent' district of Punaauia. Access to the beaches is through the former Hotel Tahiti Village. Although there are fine homes adjacent to the hotel area no one will chase you off their frontage – the general public has sunbathing and swimming rights to practically all the beaches in Tahiti. A few more km down the road will put you in Paea, which has more beaches and some of the best surfing conditions on the island. Surfing was the ancient sport of Polynesian kings, who rode the waves in to these very shores a thousand years ago. In fact, it was none other than the Tahitians who brought surfing to Hawaii, when they migrated there in the 11th and 12th centuries.

AROUND THE ISLAND

In the pre-European days Raiatea and Huahine were the most important islands in the Society group. It was only after the Europeans came that Tahiti became the centre of trade and eventually the focus for colonisation. Consequently Tahiti is the most densely populated, the most developed, and with the exception of archaeological sites (mostly on Huahine), has the most to see.

Tahiti has one main road that circles the major part of the island (Tahiti Nui), but dead-ends in the outer reaches of the smaller part of the island (Tahiti Iti). The main roads are well maintained, but tend to be narrow and overcrowded.

When driving around the island, you cross the halfway point at the Isthmus of Taravao (PK 60). From there you may either complete the circle or explore one of three dead-end roads in Tahiti Iti.

For the reader interested in an in-depth overview of the historical sights around the island, Bengt Danielsson's *Tahiti Circle Island Tour Guide* is the definitive book on the subject. Most of the information for this section was gleaned from it and I owe the author a tremendous debt for compiling facts that would otherwise be very difficult to come by. The guide is available at most bookstores in Tahiti.

The starting point for the (clockwise) tour is Papeete. The location of all sites listed on the tour is determined by their distance to or from the capital. You can pinpoint your position on the map from the red-topped 'PK' km stones along the inland or 'mountain side' of the highway. Each description of points of interest includes the 'kilometreage' to help orient the (perhaps confused) map reader.

North Coast: Papeete-Taravao

Fautaua River & Pierre Loti's Pool (2.5 km, Papeete)

Pierre Loti was the pen name for Julien Viaud, the French merchant marine whose book *The Marriage of Loti* describes the love affair of a Frenchman and a native girl (see Tahiti Literati section). The pool where he first saw the enchanting Rarahu (the novel's heroine) is located several km up the Fautaua River Valley. Unfortunately this romantic spot on the river is now covered with concrete but is marked by a bust of the author. The Bain Loti also is the trail head for a three-hour hike to the Fautaua Waterfalls (see Trekking section).

Tomb of King Pomare V (4.7 km, Arue)

A sign on the ocean side of the road marks the access road to the tomb. The Pomare line rose to power as a direct consequence of the European discovery of Tahiti. The first of the lineage, Pomare I, utilised members of the ex-*Bounty* crew who were armed with guns to defeat his enemies. Pomare I's son and successor, Pomare II, was crowned at a temple about a metre away from the site of the present-day tomb where the Protestant Church now stands. During the ceremony a *Bounty* crew member, James Morrison, reported that three human sacrifices were made on behalf of the new king.

In 1812 Pomare II became the first Tahitian convert to Christianity and after three years managed to convince the populations of Moorea and Tahiti (if necessary with the use of arms) to follow his example. In his religious zeal Pomare II constructed a temple larger than that of King Solomon out of breadfruit tree pillars, palm fronds and other local materials. The 'Royal Mission Chapel,' as it was called, was about 230 metres long (longer than St Peter's in Rome!), 18 metres wide and had the capacity to hold 6000 people. Pomare II died in 1821 at the age of 40 from the effects of alcohol and soon afterwards the Royal Mission fell into disrepair. Today a 12-sided chapel built in 1978 stands where the Royal Mission once did.

The tomb itself was constructed in 1879 for Queen Pomare, who died in 1877 after a reign of 50 years during which her country became a French colony. The

Queen's remains were removed a few years later by her son King Pomare V who, feeling that his end was near, apparently wished to occupy the mausoleum by himself. Pomare V lived on a stipend supplied by the French government, and died in 1891 at the age of 52; in true Pomare tradition, he drank himself to death. (An account of his funeral is given by Paul Gauguin in *Noa Noa*.)

Local tradition has it that the object on the tomb's roof – which misinformed guides say represents a liquor bottle (which would have been a fitting memorial to Pomare) – is actually a replica of a Greek urn.

Home of James Norman Hall (5.4 km, Arue)

Look for the old Hall residence on the mountain side of the road. Nordhoff and Hall (see Tahiti Literati section), authors of the *Bounty Trilogy, Hurricane* and *The Dark River*, probably did more to publicise Tahiti in the 20th century than did any other writers. Hall died at his Arue home in 1951 and is buried on Herai Hill just above.

Tahara'a Hotel & One Tree Hill (8.1 km)

Pull into the hotel parking lot and walk a few metres to the cliff, which affords a magnificent view of Moorea and Matavai Bay where Wallis and Cook once anchored. Wallis originally called this piece of real estate 'Skirmish Hill' because he bombarded the Tahitians gathered here with cannonballs from his ship. Cook later changed the name to 'One Tree Hill' because of the solitary *atae* tree that grew here at the time. When the American-owned hotel was built in 1968 the owners kept the Tahitian name. The Tahara'a Hotel, which hugs the bluff like a gull's nest, has recently been refurbished and continues to be popular with American visitors.

Point Venus, Museum of Discovery & Matavai Bay (10 km, Mahina)

Turn left towards the ocean at the sign marked 'Point Venus' (on the same corner as a large store). Drive about a km to the parking lot. This area has all the natural amenities – shade trees, a river, beach and exposure to cooling trade winds – and makes a wonderful picnic ground.

In the early days of Tahiti's history this tiny point of land was utilised by some of the most important visitors of that era – captains Wallis, Cook and Bligh. Until the 1820s, when Papeete became a more popular port of call, all visiting ships anchored in the area. Although Wallis, Tahiti's discoverer, landed here in 1767, it was Captain Cook's expedition in 1769 that was to give this piece of land its name.

Cook was sent by the Royal Society of England to record the transit of Venus, which would theoretically enable scientists to compute the distance between the earth and the sun – a figure that would be an invaluable tool for navigators. On 3 June 1769 the weather was good and the transit was recorded by the best instruments available at the time. Unfortunately the best equipment of the day was not accurate enough and Cook's measurements were for nought. His journey was still a success, however, because of the many new species of flora and fauna gathered by the other scientists on the trip. Cook also anchored off Matavai Bay in 1773, 1774 and 1777 during his second and third voyages of exploration.

During the *Bounty* episode in 1788, Captain Bligh also landed here, collecting breadfruit plants to use as a cheap source of food for the slave population in the West Indies. His landing became grist for Hollywood, which over the years came up with three different cinematic interpretations in 1935, 1962 and 1983. According to Danielsson, during the shooting of the 1962 *Bounty* version with Trevor Howard and Marlon Brando a sequence was filmed on Matavai Bay featuring thousands of

Tahitian extras welcoming the visitors ashore. The director, wishing to portray the Tahitians in their former glory, had the Tahitian extras don long-haired wigs and false teeth before the filming to compensate for attributes most of them no longer possessed.

Wallis and Cook are honoured by non-figurative wooden sculptures placed at Point Venus in 1969. Bligh, the third navigator to visit the area, is not remembered by any monument though Bougainville is — and he never saw Matavai Bay.

In the same area you will also note another abstract monument which Danielsson describes as a 'needle pointing to heaven.' This commemorates the arrival of the first Christian missionaries on Point Venus in 1797. Dispatched by the London Missionary Society, they abandoned their mission in 1808 and did not re-establish themselves until 1817. Though they worked actively for the British annexation of the islands, the British missionaries were eased out of Tahiti after the French takeover in 1842. The missionary era came to an end in Tahiti in 1963 when an independent Protestant church run by Polynesians was formed.

About 50 metres north-east of the Missionary Society memorial is a monument enclosed by an iron railing. According to the text on its bronze plaque, the column was erected by none other than Captain Cook in 1769 and refurbished in 1901. However, not only was the monument not built by Cook (it was a product of the local public works department), it is not located on the spot where Cook made his astronomical observations (which took place between the river and the beach).

Located in this area is the Museum of Discovery, which is housed in a thatched bamboo hut. Pay a few francs at the door and step inside to see the wax figures of Wallis, Cook and Bougainville meeting various native dignitaries. There are also memorabilia and period pieces such as a ballast bar from the real HMS Bounty and the hat worn by Charles Laughton in the 1935 MGM Bounty production. Unfortunately most of the artifacts are poorly documented in fading type.

Finally, the most visible landmark on Point Venus is the lighthouse, constructed in 1868 despite the 1867 date perhaps over-optimistically inscribed on the entrance.

Orofara Leper Colony (13.2 km, Mahina)
Prior to WW I victims of leprosy were ostracised from communities and chased into remote areas away from the population. By government decree, in 1914 the Orofara Valley was set aside as a 'leper colony' for all those in Tahiti who suffered from the dreaded disease. Until the development of sulpha drugs there was little the French Protestant mission treating the lepers here could do. Nowadays it is possible in most cases to cure the disease and allow patients to go home. According to current statistics, approximately two out of 1000 French Polynesian citizens suffer from leprosy.

Papenoo Village & Valley (17.1 km)
Papenoo is a typical rural village, the type that has rapidly disappeared since the end of WW II. Many of its homes are built in the old colonial style, with wide verandas. The Catholic and Protestant churches and 'Mairie' (city hall) are all located along the highway. Past the village, a new bridge (the longest in Tahiti) spans the Papenoo River. The Papenoo Valley, the biggest on the island, was formed by an ancient crater. The river's mouth (where the bridge is located) is the only hole in the crater wall. Continuing up the Papenoo Valley you will come to the trail head that leads across the island. (See Trekking section.)

Blowhole of Arahoho (22 km, Tiarei)
Perhaps it does not rate as one of the world's great blowholes, but it is clearly the most accessible (if not the only one) in Tahiti. Through countless years, battering surf has undercut the basalt shoreline and

eroded a passage or tube to the surface. When waves crash against the rocks, the result is a geyser-like fountain of sea water and a shower for the onlooker.

Faarumai Waterfalls (22.1 km, Tiarei)
Just past the blowhole is a marked 1.3 km dirt road leading to the three Faarumai Waterfalls. Park in the lot near a bamboo grove and walk the several hundred muddy metres to Vaimahuta, the first fall. Bring a swimsuit and some insect repellent, and try standing under the falls – an exhilarating experience. The other falls are accessible but necessitate a good hike. (See Trekking section.)

Gardens & Copra Plantation (25 km, Tiarei)
This is a private reserve but you can park and from the road see the lily ponds and accompanying flora that thrive in the area. The coconut plantation here, only one of many around Tahiti and its neighbouring islands, was once an important source of cash for the average Tahitian. Although harvesting copra (dried coconut meat) is still a vital occupation for islanders outside of Tahiti, it is of secondary importance in an economy that now relies on tourism, governmental bureaucracy and small businesses as money-earners.

Battlefield (32.5 km, Mahaena)
The annexation of Tahiti by France in 1843 sparked armed resistance among Tahitians and guerrilla warfare continued until the rebellion was crushed in 1846. The most important battle of this war was fought at Mahaena on 17 April 1844. The battlefield stretched from the beach southward to the present-day church and city hall. Heeding the advice of British sailors and French army deserters, Tahitians dug three parallel trenches and awaited their French adversaries. Two French warships did appear and a force of 441 men stormed the Tahitian position which had approximately twice the defenders but lacked the weapons of the

French. When the dust cleared 102 Tahitians were dead while the French lost only 15 men. After this blow the natives realised guerrilla warfare was the only alternative and they continued to operate from bases in the bush until their main stronghold was captured in 1846.

Bougainville's Anchorage (37.6 km, Hitiaa)
Look out to sea and note the two islets, Variararu and Oputotara. The former has a few trees and the latter just brush. Bougainville anchored at Oputotara in April 1768; a plaque at the bridge in the nearby village commemorates the event. Although cultured to the bone, Bougainville was not much of a sailor. His choice of this particular anchorage, which lacked the proper shelter and wind conditions, was not the best. He managed to lose six anchors in 10 days and nearly lost the ships as well. Believe it or not, soon after this debacle some Tahitians actually salvaged one of the anchors and gave it to the King of Bora Bora as a gift. Captain Cook later took possession of it in 1777. Bougainville will probably be best remembered for his glowing account of Tahiti, later published in France, where he lauded the Tahitians' hospitality and sexual freedom. Well versed in the classics, he called Tahiti 'New Cytheria,' after the island birthplace of the Greek goddess of love, Aphrodite. To this day, the myth lives on.

Vista of Peninsula (39 km, Hitiaa)
Splendid view of Tahiti Iti, Tahiti's panhandle.

Fa'atautia Waterfall (41.8 km, Hitiaa)
Pause at the bridge and take a few photographs. This site was chosen by American film maker John Huston to make a cinematographic version of Herman Melville's *Typee* but due to his first commercially unsuccessful Melville flick, *Moby Dick*, the scheme was abandoned.

Military Base & Junction (53 km, Taravao)
Military and police installations have
existed here since 1844 when the French
guarded the isthmus to prevent marauding
guerillas from filtering down from the
peninsula to the main part of the island.
Since then, the site has served as a
gendarmerie, an internment camp for
Germans unfortunate enough to be on the
island during WW II and, most recently, as
a French Army camp. Nearby is a large
Catholic church and also the junction for
the two roads leading to the peninsula.
Note that the north and south coast roads
do not meet – to get around the far end of
the island you must hike.

**The Peninsula's North Coast: Taravao-
Tautira**

Detour to Vista Point (0.6 km, Afaahiti)
Take the turnoff at the sign on your right,
just before the school. There are pastures
complete with grazing cattle and the
seven-km road leads to a summit. Hike the
rest and take in a gorgeous panorama of
Tahiti.

Te Anuanua Hotel (9.8 km, Pueue)
This is a highly recommended, inexpensive
hotel run by a local family.

Vaitepiha River (16.5 km, Tautira)
Great place for a swim.

Vaitepiha Bay (18 km, Tautira)
Captain Cook's second expedition almost
met its doom near Tautira in 1773. One
morning the esteemed navigator awoke to
find his two ships drifting perilously close
to the reef. Apparently the crew had been
too busy entertaining Tahitian visitors the
evening before to notice. The ships
eventually did run aground, but were
saved by smaller boats that kedged the
larger vessels off the reef. Cook lost
several anchors in the confusion. In 1978,
by sheer luck, one of the anchors was
located and brought to the surface. The
event was properly celebrated by locals

and the crew of movie producer David
Lean who was on location to promote a
new version of the *Bounty* episode.
Although the film was never made, the
anchor can be seen at the Musee de Tahiti
et des Isles.

This bucolic setting was also the scene
of a confrontation between the British and
the Spanish. Angered at the English
presence in the Pacific (which the Spanish
felt was theirs to plunder) the Viceroy of
Peru was ordered by his King to send a
ship to Tahiti. He promptly sent the
Aguila, commanded by Boenecha, which
after having the misfortune of striking a
reef, anchored in a lagoon about three km
from Tautira village and formally 'took
possession' of Tahiti for the King of
Spain. Less than a year later, Cook, on his
second voyage of discovery, wound up in
the same vicinity and soon heard about
the landing of the dastardly Spanish. In
1774 Boenecha returned to the area with
two Franciscan priests in an effort to give
the savages a little religion. The mission
failed miserably. Captain Boenecha soon
died and the priests, scared witless of the
Tahitians, erected a veritable fortress to
keep the curious natives away. The *Aguila*
returned at the end of 1775 with provisions
but the priests would have none of the
missionary life and gladly sailed back to
Peru.

Cook came back to Tautira on his third
voyage in 1777 and found the padre's
quarters still in good condition. The house
was fitted with a crucifix which bore the
inscription 'Christus vincit Carolus III
imperat 1774.' On the reverse side of the
cross Cook ordered his carpenter to carve
'Tertius Rex Annis 1767, 69, 73, 74, & 77.'
By this time, Bengt Danielsson writes,
'both England and Spain had realised that
Tahiti was an economically as well as
strategically worthless island and gave up
their costly shows of force.'

One hundred years later Tautira was
the temporary abode of Robert Louis
Stevenson, who anchored the *Casco* here
in 1888 (see Tahiti Literati). He was taken

in by local royalty and stayed for about two months, calling Tahiti a 'Garden of Eden.' Although on assignment for the *New York Sun* to write about the cruise he spent his time in Tautira working on *The Master of Ballantrae*, a Scottish horror story. Upon returning to England, Stevenson's mother sent a silver communion service to the local Protestant church, where it is still being used.

The Peninsula: Taravao-Teahuupoo

Research Station (0.5 km, Afaahiti)

This atmospheric research station was constructed during the 'International Geophysical Year, 1957-1958' to study the ionosphere.

Zane Grey's Fishing Camp (7.3 km, Toahotu)

Although the author of *Riders of the Purple Sage* and 60 other pulp westerns spent his life cranking out stories about the old American West, his real passion in life was deep-sea fishing. From 1928 to 1930 he spent many months in Tahiti with his cronies catching marlin, mahimahi, sailfish and other sport fish. Like Melville's protagonist in *Moby Dick*, Grey dreamed of landing his own version of the white whale and on 16 May 1930 he finally did – a 4¼ metre, 450 kg-plus 'silver marlin' that probably would have weighed 90 kg more had not the sharks ripped off so much flesh. Describing this episode in *Tales of Tahitian Waters*, Grey gives us an insight into French Colonial mentality. Grey relates that French officials had the local chief spy on the Americans because they thought the fishermen might actually be surveying the area for the US government which perhaps had designs of taking over Tahiti as a naval base. Said Grey, 'The idea of white men visiting Tahiti for something besides French liquors, the native women, or to paint the tropical scenery had been exceedingly hard to assimilate.'

Maui's Footprints on the Reef (8.5 km, Vairao)

Tradition has it that on this very spot the great Polynesian hero Maui slowed down the sun in order to provide time for the Tahitians to cook their food before it got dark. Maui accomplished this by braiding a rope of pubic hair from his sister Hina, lassoing the sun, and tying the unwieldy ball down to a boulder on the beach. To prove the tale Maui's footprints are still visible on the reef.

CNEXO Oceanographic Research Station (10.4 km, Vairao)

The ponds you see here are for breeding shrimp – one of the many ambitious projects of CNEXO (Centre National pour l'Exploitation des Oceans), a French government agency.

Last Refuge of the Nature Men (18 km, Teahuupoo)

Years ago the 'nature men,' as Danielsson refers to them, were a common fixture throughout Tahiti, but as civilisation marched on this remote area became their last refuge. The most well-known of these rugged individuals, who perhaps bore a strong resemblance to the American underground comic book character 'Mr Natural,' was Ernest Darling. According to Danielsson, Darling 'lived stark naked, slept on the ground with his head pointing north, and produced an endless stream of pamphlets, extolling the virtues of nudism, vegetarianism, abstinence, pacifism, Christian Socialism and phonetic spelling.'

West Coast Road: Taravao-Papeete

Home of Robert Keable (55.5 km, Papeari)

Look carefully among the mango trees on the hill and you will see the former home of English writer Robert Keable. Although not a household word today, Keable produced two religious novels, *Simon Called Peter* and *Recompense*, which sold a combined total of 600,000 copies in the

Top: Re-enactment of the crowning of a prince during Tiurai celebrations (RK)
Left: Basket weaving contest during Tiurai (RK)
Right: Tahitian warrior at Tiurai celebrations (RK)

Top: 19th century vanilla plantation house in Moorea (RK)
Left: Tomb of Pomare IV in Tahiti (RK)
Right: Lighthouse at Point Venus, Tahiti (RK)

1920s. Obsessed with the question of why Tahiti and Tahitian women held so much attraction for white men, he provided his own answers in two more books *Tahiti, Isle of Dreams* and *Numerous Treasure*. Keable's well-maintained home is in its original 1920s condition.

Debarkation Point of Ancient Tahitians (52 km, Papeari)

Traditional accounts say that this was the first place the ancient Polynesians settled over a thousand years ago. Because of this, families chiefly from this district have always had the highest prestige among their counterparts in the other districts of Tahiti. The present-day village is known for its beautiful gardens and roadside produce stands.

Botanical Gardens & Gauguin Museum (51.2 km, Motu Ovini)

The gardens were established in 1919 by Harrison Smith, a physics professor who at age 37 left the Massachusetts Institute of Technology to dedicate the rest of his life to botany in Tahiti. He introduced a variety of tropical shrubs, trees and flowers from throughout the world to the islands, some of which became important local products. My favourite among these is the huge, delectable grapefruit known as the pomplemousse, which originated in Borneo. Smith did not merely putter around in his own garden but generously gave seeds and cuttings to Tahitian farmers to help them improve their own crops. After his death in 1947 the garden was willed to another botanist and through the help of American philanthropist Cornelius Crane was given to the public.

The massive garden is laced with footpaths that wend their way through hectares of well-tended palms, hibiscus, elephant ears, bamboo, bananas and many other species. There are also several Galapagos turtles brought to Tahiti in the 1930s which were given to author Charles Nordhoff's children.

Located on the garden grounds is a modern, circular building – the Gauguin Museum – with exhibits chronicling the life of Tahiti's most famous former resident. The walls are covered with documents and photographs from the Gauguin era, along with reproductions of his works. Ironically, in the Gauguin Museum there are very few original works or objects from Gauguin's own life. For sale at the gift shop are excellent reproductions of his paintings and the works of other artists who resided on the island.

Outside the museum note the two-metre-tall *tiki* (statue) from Raivavae in the Austral group. Those in the know say it has a curse attached to it, as do many tikis removed from their original surroundings.

Although modern-day Tahiti is very different than it was during Paul Gauguin's time, the joyous and perplexing moods of Tahitians that he captured on canvas are still displayed today on every street corner in Papeete.

Gauguin Museum Restaurant (50.5 km, Papeari)

Located on the ocean side, the restaurant is excellent but somewhat expensive.

Vaihiria River & Lake (48 km, Mataiea)

The Vaihiria River originates from the lake of the same name – Tahiti's only lake. Located 500 metres above sea level, it is bounded on the north by 1000-metre cliffs which make up the southern wall of the Papenoo crater. The lake is known among locals for its large eels and nearby plantations of *fe'i* (mountain bananas). It is accessible with the aid of a guide. (For more information, see Trekking section.)

Mataiea Village (46.5 km, Mataiea)

After living briefly in Papeete, Paul Gauguin moved to this village in October of 1891 and lived here until May of 1893. He rented a bamboo hut, found a vahine and painted such masterpieces as *Hina Tefatou* (The Museum of Modern Art, New York), *Ia Orana Maria* (The Metropolitan Museum of Art, New York),

Fatata te Miti (The National Gallery of Art, Washington, DC), *Manao Tupapau* (Albright-Knox Art Gallery, Buffalo), *Reverie* (The William Rockhill Nelson Gallery of Art, Kansas City) and *Under the Pandanus* (The Minneapolis Institute of Art).

Twenty-three years later, when Somerset Maugham came to the village culling information about Gauguin's life for his novel *The Moon and Sixpence*, he discovered three painted glass doors in the wooden bungalow belonging to Gauguin's landlord. These paintings by the great artist had never been discovered. Most of the paintings had been mutilated by children's play but Maugham picked the best one up for 200 francs and painstakingly shipped it back to Europe. Near the end of his life he sold the forgotten door at Sotheby's for a cool £13,000. (For more about Maugham in Tahiti see Tahiti Literati section.)

Rupert Brooke's Love Nest (44 km, Mataiea)

Shortly before WW I Rupert Brooke jumped on a boat in San Francisco and headed for Tahiti 'to hunt for lost Gauguins.' He ended up in Mataiea, rented a bungalow, and instead of discovering lost French painters found his first and only true love. Mamua inspired one of his best poems, 'Tiare Tahiti.' Brooke eventually left Tahiti with a heavy heart and several years later died on a hospital ship off Gallipoli, a casualty of the war. His beloved Mamua fell three years after that, a victim of Spanish influenza. (See Tahiti Literati section).

Atimaono Golf Course (41 km, Papara)

Though today this area is a golf course (see section on Sports) the cotton plantation that once covered what today are fairways and sand traps had a tremendous impact on Tahiti's population and history. The story begins not in Tahiti but in the United States which in the early 1860s was in the midst of a bloody civil war. This war not only caused bloodshed in the States but in Europe created a shortage of the cotton that usually came from the southern USA. The demand for this commodity gave Scottish wine merchant William Stewart, who made a living importing liquor to the South Pacific, the idea of growing cotton in Tahiti. He acquired land in Atimaono, the only area in Tahiti capable of large-scale agricultural development, and with the help of blackbirders (slave traders), he recruited labour. This did not work too well, so coolie labour from China was used and thus the seeds of the powerful Chinese community in Tahiti were planted. Working conditions were atrocious and violence tempered by the guillotine was the rule of the day.

Despite the awful circumstances, by 1867 1000 hectares of high-grade cotton were planted and the harvest lived up to Stewart's dreams. In the meantime he had built a huge villa and spent his evenings as the king of the roost, entertaining Tahitian high society. However, there was a catch. The American Civil War had ended and with it the shortage of cotton from the United States ended. Stewart could not compete with his American counterparts who were geographically much closer to Europe, and he plummeted into bankruptcy. He died at the young age of 48. About half the Chinese coolies elected to stay and the rest is history.

Site of Marae Mahaiatea (39.2 km, Papara)

The access road to the ruins of this once great temple is posted on the highway. Today it is only a huge pile of boulders but early European visitors (such as Captain Cook) were astounded by its dimensions (about 90 metres long, 29 metres wide and 15 metres high) and its architecture. Not only did the builders need a considerable amount of skill to construct the temple, they had to do so without the benefit of iron tools. Danielsson claims it was once the most spectacular monument in Tahiti. The temple's fall into decay is not only the fault of nature – apparently the old temple was used by William Stewart as a source of stones for his building projects down at the cotton plantation a few km away. In the words of J C Beaglehole, the great biographer of Cook whom Danielsson quotes in describing the fate of the marae, 'Nature and human stupidity combine as usual to wipe out the diverse signs of human glory.'

Protestant Church & US Civil War Memorial (36 km, Papara)

In the graveyard of this Tahitian Church lie the remains of a former US Consul and Yankee hero of the Civil War. The inscription on the stone tells the story of Dorence Atwater who at age 16 joined the Union Army, was captured by rebel scouts and served time in three Confederate prisons until he was sent to a hospital where he ended up as a clerk recording the deaths of Federal prisoners. Fearing the Confederates were not keeping accurate records, he copied the lists and escaped, bringing them to the attention of the Federal government. Atwater was buried here because in 1875 he wed the beautiful 'princess' Moetia of the local chief's family which had ruled the district for generations.

Border between Papara & Paea (30 km)

The districts of Paea and Papara have the least amount of rainfall and are among the most desirable areas in Tahiti to live. Note the fine homes on the coast (mostly owned by whites) and the quiet lagoon and beaches, sheltered by a barrier reef.

Paroa Cave (28.5 km, Paea)

This cave, always a stop on the visitor's itinerary, has no traditional importance. Its only meagre significance is that it is an optical illusion – it seems to be smaller than it is.

Marae Arahurahu (22.5 km, Paea)

Danielsson writes that this particular marae (a short walk off the main road from a Chinese grocery) had no great historical importance, but it did capture the imagination of Dr Sinoto of the Bishop Museum enough so that he completely reconstructed the shrine. The rectangular pyramid is about the size of a tennis court and has a flat top with a wooden platform where animal and human offerings were left for the gods. The marae has been used during the Tiurai festival in July as a stage for re-enactments of ancient rituals such as the 'Crowning of a King' ceremony or similar events. The temple is situated in a lush valley bordered by steep cliffs.

Irihonu Craft Center (20 km, Paea)

At the mouth of the Orofero River are three buildings housing the workshops of artisans (all members of the Paea Craft Association) who still practise the traditional arts of the islands – woodcarving, mat-weaving and a skill introduced by missionaries – quilting. The varied arts and crafts are on sale at the centre, which is supported by the local Paea government. In the past few years there has been a resurgence of interest in the old Polynesian arts, a trend that will hopefully check the disappearance of traditional skills.

Near the crafts centre is a popular surfing spot. Surfing is a sport the Tahitians have practised since time immemorial and brought with them to Hawaii. During the missionary years surfing was prohibited (surfboards were ridden naked in those days) and it wasn't until the 1960s, after Tahitians had visited Hawaii by plane, that the sport actually made a comeback. The same beach was also the site of a marae where in 1777 Captain Cook witnessed a human sacrifice.

This area was also the scene of an important battle in 1815 that pitted Pomare II, by then a Christian convert, against the heathen forces of the Tevai Uta clan. Pomare's well-armed Christian soldiers, aided by white mercenaries, overran their adversaries but with true Christian mercy spared the enemy from unbridled revenge. Pomare spared human life but unfortunately all of the artistic treasures – the wooden and stone carvings – were either tossed into the fire or destroyed, leaving future generations with very little in the way of Tahitian art. One of the results of this episode is that today's artisans carve tikis which are copies of works from the Marquesas Islands or of the New Zealand Maoris.

Musee de Tahiti et des Iles (15.1 km, Punaauia)

Opened in 1978, the museum is an excellent introduction to Tahiti and the entire spectrum of French Polynesian culture. You can get there by taking a right turn (coming from Papeete) at the sign posted at the junction of the gas station and market and continuing toward the beach for another km or so. Prior to the damage caused by the cyclones of May '83, this was perhaps the finest and most modern museum in the South Pacific. Although the artifacts remain in good condition, serious damage was caused to the roof and electrical wiring system. Some of the displays at the government-operated facility were opened to the public in December '83, and the permanent exhibition should be reopened by now. It will consist of four sections:

'Milieu Natural' – flora, fauna, geology and Polynesian migration exhibits. Many of the displays include sophisticated, electrically operated diagrams and instructional aides.

'Traditional Polynesian Culture' – homes, costumes, religion, games, dance, musical instruments and ornaments.

'Post-Contact Era' – displays illustrating Cook, Bougainville, Wallis, Pomare dynasty, missionary period and Chinese population.

'Outdoor Exhibits' – botanical garden consisting of plants that Tahitians brought with them (such as taro, 'ava, yams, medicinal herbs) and the Canoe Room displaying traditional outrigger and dugout canoes.

In addition to the museum's exhibits of traditional arts and crafts there is a wonderful collection of paintings and prints. Most of these will be available for viewing in the Exhibition Building which will have rotating shows ranging from artists like Webber (Captain Cook's artist) to modern-day Tahitian painters, sculptors and potters who otherwise would not have the means of displaying their works. Exhibitions will not be limited to local art but will show works from throughout the Pacific and the rest of the world.

The building will also be the home of special events such as demonstrations of tapa making, mat weaving, instrument making, traditional dances and exhibits illustrating the latest archaeological excavations.

No visitor to Tahiti with an interest in the island's culture should miss the museum. Hours are 9 am to 6 pm daily except Monday.

Punaru'u Valley (14.8 km, Punaauia)

Beyond the bridge was once a fortress built by the French during the Tahitian uprising of 1844-46. The site is now used as a TV relay station. The road up the valley leads to a trail (see Trekking section) to the Tamanu Plateau where oranges grow in profusion. In the 19th century Tahiti was a large exporter of oranges to New Zealand and – believe it or not – to California.

2+2=4 Primary School & Site of Gauguin Home (1.26 km, Punaauia)

A 19th-century French landowner donated the land for the school and had the above mathematical equation inscribed at the entrance. According to Danielsson, the planter, dubious about the propriety of introducing the French educational system to Tahiti, figured that if nothing else the children would learn at least one thing of value.

Just south of the school, in an area now subdivided, Paul Gauguin lived in a fine home from 1897 to 1901 and produced about 60 paintings. Among these are *Where Do We Come From* (The Museum of Fine Arts, Boston), *Faa Iheihe* (Tate Gallery, London) and *Two Tahitian Women* (The Metropolitan Museum, New York).

Lagoonarium (11 km, Punaauia)
This is a decent restaurant combined with a small aquarium. Open daily (except Monday), noon to 2 pm and after 7 pm.

'Super Highway' Entrance (7.8 km, Punaauia)
At this point the motorist can either take a modern four-lane freeway and zoom back to Papeete, or travel down the old coastal highway.

Beachcomber Hotel (7.2 km, Punaauia)
The site of the present-day Beachcomber Hotel (which has one of the best cuisines on the island) is called Tata'a Point. In times past it was a holy place where the souls of the dead were said to depart to the nether world.

Faaa International Airport (5.5 km)
Faaa Airport is as modern as any in the world, but still has distinct Tahitian touches like barefoot kids, rotund Tahitian women selling shell *leis* (necklaces) and perhaps an unattended dog sleeping near the ticket counter. The present-day airport's 3.5-km runway was constructed by filling in a lagoon. Prior to its completion in 1961 Tahiti was served by passenger vessels and New Zealand TEAL flying boats. (For more information on airport facilities see the Getting Around section in this chapter.)

TREKKING
Upon your arrival in Tahiti the verdant hills beckon but venturing into the bush can be a dangerous proposition unless you know what you are doing and where you are going. Torrential rain can swell streams into rivers and 'easy-to-find' trails can be overgrown with vegetation in

no time. It's always best for the serious hiker to be accompanied by a guide. In many instances it's also best to rent a four-wheel-drive vehicle to get to the trail head.

Despite the requirements, Tahiti has a variety of excellent trails and guides for hire. Here are seven treks of varying difficulty. Many, but not all, require guides:

Mataiea-Lake Vaihiria-Papenoo This two-day, across-the-island hike via Lake Vaihiria (Tahiti's only lake) begins on the south coast, crosses the island's ancient volcanic crater and ends in Papenoo on the north coast. Allow 45 minutes by four-wheel-drive vehicle to the Mataiea trail head. Hikers should be in good physical condition and a guide is required.

Mt Aorai Trek begins at the end of the Belvedere restaurant road (near Papeete). This is a two-day hike and a guide is required. Small *fares* have been constructed to shelter hikers along the trail.

Fautaua Waterfall For this day trip up the Fautaua Valley take an ordinary car to Bain Loti (of Pierre Loti fame) and walk three hours to the waterfall. A guide is not necessary but permission is needed from the Service des Eaux et Forets.

One Thousand Springs hike This is a comparatively easy hike and no guide is required. Take Mahinarama Road (near the Tahara'a Hotel) to the end (about five km) and walk two hours to the springs. From this juncture it is possible to climb Mt Orohena (Tahiti's highest) but a guide is required for such an undertaking.

Plateau of Oranges (Punaruu Valley) Take a car to Punaauia (about 15 km from Papeete) and enter the Punaruu Valley road to the trail head (one to two km by car). Walk to Tamanu Plateau – an eight-hour hike. Trekkers should be in good shape and a guide is required.

Lava Tubes Start at PK 40 (east coast) and four-wheel it about eight km. It's a two-hour walk to the Lava Tubes. The walk is easy but a guide is required.

Te Pari-Tahiti Iti hike This is a fairly rigorous hike around the far end of Tahiti, or 'Tahiti-Iti' as it is known. The pavement ends at Teahuupoo on the south side and Tautira on the north side but a trail along the coast connects the two roads. Get a guide for this and give yourself three days.

PLACES TO STAY

The hotels listed here are considered good value for their price range. Hotel reservations can be made through your travel agent; lodging in the less expensive places can be reserved by writing directly to the hotel. In most cases there are vacancies year round with the exception of July. During the Bastille Day celebrations (starting 14 July and lasting until August), it is virtually impossible to find a hotel room in Papeete. If you want to avoid crowds, this is not the time to come to Tahiti.

Places to Stay – bottom end

Just a 10-minute walk from Papeete, the *Mahina Tea* (tel 2-00-97) is your basic family-run, pension-style lodging. There are no frills or luxury about this place, but it is clean, although reports are that local roosters can be aggravatingly noisy. It has 16 rooms with bathrooms, some 'studios,' hot water from 6 pm to 11 pm. Rates are 2300 cfp for a single, 2500 cfp for a double and 4000 cfp for a studio. Rates drop 300-400 cfp if the guest stays more than one night! Write Vallon de Sainte-Amelie, PO Box 17, Papeete.

Le Lagoon Hotel (tel 2-98-46) has 14 rooms, a common bathroom and no hot water. Other rooms are available with private bathrooms. Rates are 2500 cfp per night for a single or double (common bath) or 3500 cfp per night (private bath). The address is Chemin Vicinal de Patutoa, PO Box 635, Papeete.

The rock-bottom, bargain-basement special in Tahiti is the *OTAC* (Territorial Hostel Center). It offers clean, dormitory-style accommodation. There are 18 rooms

with three beds in each and three rooms with two beds. The cost is 1000 cfp for the first night, 800 cfp for each additional night. The centre does not have kitchen facilities but there is a canteen and a meal can be had for around 350 cfp. The doors are locked at midnight. For reservations write M Jeffrey Salmon, Office Territorial d'Action Culturel, PO Box 1709, Papeete. (You must have a student ID or youth hostel card.)

Pensions Staying with families is an inexpensive and often enriching alternative to hotels. Sometimes it affords you a chance to see a side of Tahiti you would otherwise never experience. Note that rates and services listed below are more subject to change than is typical accommodation. The families marked with an asterisk (*) have been recommended as stand-outs.

*Fare Oviri** (tel 8-31-88) has one bungalow with two bedrooms (maximum four persons), kitchen, bathroom with hot water, television and white sand beach. The minimum stay is six nights – one or two persons 30,000 cfp, three persons 35,000 cfp, four persons 40,000 cfp. For additional nights the rate is 6000 cfp per night for one or two persons, 7000 cfp per night for three persons, 8000 cfp per night for four persons. A deposit of 5000 cfp is needed for a confirmed reservation. Transfers are available on request between the airport and the residence (one way) for 1000 cfp. The address is PK 18.2, Punaauia. For reservations call or write Mme Anne Ribet, PO Box 3486, Papeete. Reservations are not needed at *Chez Fineau-Tautau* (tel 3-74-99); no children are accepted. There are two rooms, single or double. Rates are 1500 cfp per day for one person, 3000 cfp per day for two people. There is a 10% discount for stays of two days or more. The address is Angle Rue de General Castelneau et Rue de Pont Neuf No 4 (second house on the right on Pont Neuf), Papeete.

Chez Heimata et Marc (tel 2-83-71) has two single or double rooms and a common bathroom with hot water. Rates include breakfast; one person is 3500 cfp per day, two persons 4500 cfp per day. Children aged five to 12 are 800 cfp per day, 13 and over 1000 cfp per day. The address is Tipaerui-quartier Smith (300 metres after the Matavai Hotel on the right), Papeete. Contact M Marc Faaruia at that address for reservations.

Activities at *Chez Tihoti* (tel 3-80-26) include an around-the-island tour, lagoon tour and deep-sea fishing. It has one single or double room and a bathroom with hot water. The cost for one or two persons is 3000 cfp per day; breakfast is 400 cfp; lunch and dinner 1600 cfp. The address is PK 12.5, Punaauia (mountain side).

Chez Mareva Ura* (tel 3-98-31) has one single or double room with a private bathroom and hot water. Rates include breakfast; for one person the cost is 4500 cfp, two persons 5500 cfp. The address is PK 11.2, Punaauia (ocean side, next to the Auberge du Pacifique. For reservations write or call Mme Tehani Sylvain, PO Box 349, Papeete.

Chez Nicole (tel 2-48-00) has three single or double rooms with a common bathroom. Rates include breakfast; for one person the cost is 2500 cfp per day, two persons 3000 cfp per day, an extra person 1000 cfp. The address is Sainte-Amelie St, Papeete (sixth entrance on the right after the snack bar Chez Yvonne). For reservations call or write Mme Nicole Sorgniard, PO Box 9272, Papeete.

Chez Solange (tel 8-21-07) has two single or double rooms, a common bathroom with hot water and access to the beach. With breakfast, the rates are one or two persons 2500 cfp per day, children (ages five to 12) 500 cfp per day. Dinner is 700 to 1000 cfp per person. The address is PK 15 (ocean side), Punaauia, across the road from the Mobil station Raumanu. For reservations call or write Mme Solange Vandeputte, PO Box 4230, Papeete.

Chez Maire asks a deposit of 4000 cfp for confirmed reservations – women or couples only. Transfers are available on request. Accommodation is one single or double room and a bathroom with hot water. Rates including breakfast are: one woman 4000 cfp per day, a couple or two women 5000 cfp per day. The address is Mahina St, the same street the Super Mahina store is on (1.6 km from the CEA). For reservations call or write Mme Ginette Maire, PO Box 11188, Mahina.

Accommodation at *Chez Michel et Armelle* (tel 7-11-48) is one double room with a common bathroom (including hot water). Electricity is available from 6 pm to 10 pm. There is also a chalet with a kitchen, bathroom and living room (maximum four persons). Rates (with breakfast) for a double are 3000 cfp for one person, 4000 cfp for two and 1000 extra cfp for an additional person. Children ages five to 12 get a 50% discount. The chalet costs 5000 cfp per day for one or two persons, 1000 cfp per extra bed. The address is PK 7, Pueu, Plateau of Taravao. For reservations write or call M Michel Riviere, Plateau of Taravao, PK 7.

Te Anuanua Hotel* (tel 7-12-54 or 7-13-87) has two double seaside bungalows with bathrooms and one deluxe air-conditioned bungalow with a bathroom and hot water. A double is 3500 cfp per day for one or two persons (children five to 12 are 500 cfp per day), 10,000 cfp per day for an air-conditioned bungalow (children five to 12 are 1000 cfp per day). The restaurant is open Monday through Sunday (except Thursdays). Breakfast costs 200-300 cfp, lunch 850 cfp and dinner (cold meal) 700 cfp. The address is PK 10 (ocean side), Pueu. For reservations call or write to Mme Stella Lehartel.

Places to Stay – middle

Climat de France Punaauia (tel 3-08-01) is located on Punaauia Hill near the airport. It has 40 air-conditioned rooms. Rates are 8400 cfp for a single and 10,900 cfp for a double. Write PO Box 576, Papeete.

Matavai (tel 2-67-67) was formerly the Holiday Inn but as far as I am concerned, once a Holiday Inn always a Holiday Inn. The 146-room hotel is located on the outskirts of town and is popular with airlines who put put their flight crews up for the night there. Awful architecture. Prices are 8000 cfp for a single and 10,600 cfp for a double. Write PO Box 32, Papeete.

Royal Papeete (tel 2-01-29) is situated directly opposite the waterfront or 'quay' in the midst of Papeete's entertainment and shopping district. In its day it was one of the finer hotels but now is known mainly as the home of *La Cave*, one of the best nightclubs going. The 85-room Royal Papeete is not luxurious but is certainly adequate and is good for business people who need to stay 'in town.' Prices begin at 5600 cfp for a single and 5900 cfp for a double. The address is PO Box 919, Papeete.

Located about two km from the heart of Papeete, the *Hotel Tahiti* (tel 2-95-50) was also one of the best resorts around in its heyday. With 92 rooms and 18 bungalows, a swimming pool and an excellent restaurant, it is a good choice for the visitor who wants good accommodation but doesn't need the lap of luxury. Rates are 6500 cfp for a single and 7000 cfp for a double. The address is PO Box 416, Papeete.

The *Princess Heiata* (tel 2-81-05) is best known as an after-hours club on the weekends for revellers who don't think the party is over when the nightclubs close down. It has 25 rooms and 11 bungalows and is located about five km from Papeete going east towards Pirae. Prices are 5800 cfp for a single and 6600 cfp for a double. Write PO Box 5003, Papeete.

Located next to the Beachcomber about seven km from Papeete, *Te Puna Bel Air* (tel 2-82-24) is reasonably priced and adequate. It has 48 modern motel-style rooms and 28 thatched bungalows with overhead fans. The hotel has a freshwater pond-cum-swimming pool with ferocious-looking but perfectly harmless

eels. It also has spacious gardens, a good restaurant and is near the beach. Sundays feature a Tahitian feast followed by dancing to a local band. Prices start at 5500 cfp for a single and 6500 cfp for a double. The address is PO Box 354, Papeete.

Hotel Pacific (tel 3-72-82) is a recently renovated hotel (formerly the Kon Tiki), moderately priced and located in the heart of Papeete on the Boulevard Pomare. It used to be pretty tacky but is now quite acceptable. There are 44 rooms; rates are 6000 cfp for a single and 6500 cfp for a double. Write PO Box 111, Papeete.

Places to Stay – top end

Beachcomber (tel 2-51-10), a 200-room resort located two km from Faaa Airport and eight km from Papeete, is a compromise between city and town – close enough to enjoy Papeete but far away enough to avoid the hustle. It is located on the water and features the usual assortment of water sports and cruises as well as standard rooms or air-conditioned over-the-water bungalows. Over the past several years management has poured $5 million into refurbishing the rooms; more recently the bar/restaurant and conference hall have been totally revamped. A new terrace restaurant is also under construction and in general cuisine is much improved. Prices begin at 15,400 cfp for a single and 17,900 for a double. The address is PO Box 6014, Faaa, Tahiti.

Located about nine km from Papeete (just down the road from the Beachcomber), the *Maeva Beach* (tel 2-80-42) was one of the first luxury hotels in French Polynesia. It has 230 rooms, one of the best restaurants on the island (the Gauguin) and is near the beach. It feels more like a European hotel than any resort on the island. Prices begin at 11,900 cfp for a single and 12,900 cfp for a double. Write Box 6008, Faaa Airport.

Hotel Tahara'a (tel 8-11-22) is perched on a summit named 'One Tree Hill' by Captain Cook and overlooks historic

Matavai Bay. The hotel is located on the boundary of the Arue district about eight km outside Papeete. Below the Tahara'a is a gorgeous black sand beach. After a recent hotel strike that crippled Tahiti, it was reopened in September of 1984 and given a $2 million renovation which modernised every one of its 200 rooms. The largest American-owned hotel in French Polynesia, the Tahara'a is very popular with folks from the United States. It has a superb view and a nice feeling of isolation, even though the hotel is just off the road. Write Box 1015, Papeete, Tahiti. Rates start at 13,300 cfp for a single and 15,400 cfp for a double.

Located in the 'suburb' of Pirae, the *Royal Tahitian* (tel 2-81-15) has 45 rooms with an ocean view and a very nice black sand beach. Rooms start at 13,100 cfp (US$85) for a single and 13,900 cfp (US$90) for a double. Write PO Box 5001, Pirae.

On Tetiaroa there is an atoll resort owned by the inimitable Marlon Brando. The islet is a 15-minute, 40-km flight from Faaa Airport in Tahiti. Tetiaroa was originally a royal refuge for the Pomare family in times of tribal war and for ancient religious rites (as archaeological sites attest). Brando purchased it in 1965 for his own use and opened it to the public in 1973. The address is PO Box 2418, Papeete (tel 2-63-02 in Tahiti).

PLACES TO EAT

One of the best things about Tahiti is its restaurants. Thanks to the discerning French palate, Papeete is the only town in the South Pacific (with the possible exception of Noumea) where it is actually difficult to find a lousy restaurant. The main cuisines in Tahiti are French, Tahitian, Vietnamese and Chinese or various combinations thereof. Prices range from reasonable to very expensive – US$5 to US$50 per person. Those listed represent the cost of an average meal.

Auberge Landaise (Boulevard Pomare). French cuisine, 5000 cfp, considered the best French restaurant in Papeete.

Le Madrepore (Boulevard Pomare in the Vaima Center). French, 4000 cfp.

Le Mandarin (Rue des Ecoles). Chinese, 2000-3000 cfp.

Jade Palace (Rue Jeanne d'Arc, Vaima Center). Chinese, 3000-4000 cfp.

Moana Iti (Boulevard Pomare). French-Tahitian, 2000-3000 cfp.

Le Baie d'Along (Avenue du Prince Hanoi). Fine Vietnamese food, 1500-2500 cfp.

Le Pescadou (one block from Vaima Center on Rue A M Javouhey). Italian, specialises in pizza – lively ambience and the best pizza in town, 1000 cfp.

Pizzeria (Italian) (Boulevard Pomare). Good pizza but lacks the atmosphere of Le Pescadou, 1000 cfp.

Waikiki (Rue A Leboucher). Good, inexpensive Chinese-Tahitian food, 1200 cfp.

Polyself (Rue Gauguin next to the Bank of Polynesia). Caters to the lunchtime office crowd – Chinese-Tahitian cafeteria-style food but consistently good, 800 cfp.

Places to Eat Outside Papeete

Pirae *Le Belvedere* is perched on a mountainside near Papeete (free transportation is available, call 2-73-44) – great view day or night. It serves French food at 2500 cfp and specialises in Fondue Bourguignonne (meat fondue).

Pamatai *La Chaumiere* has an oceanside view. They offer French cuisine at 3000 cfp.

Punaauia *Coco's* serves seafood at 3000 cfp and is located near the ocean (PK 13). There is also an American-style bar, *L'Auberge du Pacifique*, offering seafood at 3000 cfp (PK 11.2).

Faaa *Le Gauguin* is located at the Maeva Beach Hotel (PK 7.5). The cuisine is French at 5000 cfp.

Papara *Le Petit Mousse* (PK 32.5), constructed on the water, makes for nice Sunday afternoon dining outdoors. It serves North African food at 2500 cfp.

Mataiea *Le Vahoata* (PK 42.9) is famous for its Tahitian feasts on Sunday. Food is Tahitian at 2500 cfp.

Papeari *Musee Gauguin* (PK 60) has good French food and pleasant surroundings at 2500 cfp.

ENTERTAINMENT

Papeete by night: Moonglow and a freighter's lights reflect from the rippling waters of the harbour. A warm south-east trade wind blows through the narrow streets and ruffles the bright print dresses of vahines as they walk in pairs towards the neon signs.

On the street, young sailors with crew cuts and tight-fitting jeans leer at the girls, banter in French and puff away at Gauloises cigarettes. Behind them, the pulsating disco beat of the Blackjack Club blares into the night. A painted, miniskirted Tahitian in stilt-like platform shoes stands at the doorway and peers into the street.

Across the Boulevard Pomare, on the quay, the American yachts are moored neatly in a row. Inside the lighted cabins you can make out the figures of people eating dinner and sipping wine from plastic cups. Occasionally a denim-clad youth will slip out of a darkened yacht, cross the street and disappear into the maze of lights and people.

Down the Boulevard Pomare, near the bus stop, several old women with sleeping babies at their sides sit cross-legged on pandanus mats and weave crowns of pungent Tiare Tahiti beneath fluorescent street lamps. Later they will peddle their fragrant creations in restaurants, night clubs, bars and streets.

Over at the Pitate Club, across from the Monument de Gaulle, the band has started to play a Tahitian-style fox trot and couples are slowly filing in. At the bar sit four crew members of a Chilean naval ship. The young men, who have been two months at sea, ogle the women and squirm self-consciously on their orange plastic seats. The Tahitian women eye them; some whisper to their boyfriends that they will try to hustle a few drinks from the *popa'a* (foreigners).

Clubs range from sleazy servicemen's clip joints to posh discos. However, before you step out, prepare to spend some cash. The cheapest beer in town is at least 300 cfp, and the price for a cocktail ranges from 1000-1500 cfp. On a weekend night most clubs will extract a cover charge of about 1000 cfp, which includes a drink. Papeete is a small town, and most places are within several minutes' walking distance of each other.

Undoubtedly the friendliest places in town are the rollicking, working-class bars where the common people come to unwind with conversation and a few beers. The bars are noisy, crowded, smoke-filled dens that usually have a trio or quartet hammering away on ukeleles and guitars. These places will seem formidable at first because of the mass of people packed inside. Once you're in and flash a few smiles, however, the locals will be quite amiable.

Someone will most likely buy you a beer

and ask where you're from and if you're married. For some reason, Tahitians are extremely curious about one's marital status. If you have no spouse, they will shake their heads and say, 'Aita matai (no good), maybe you find a nice vahine from Tahiti.' You might also be questioned about a person they have met from the same area. 'You know Jimmy from Los Angeles? He come here two years ago. He nice man.'

Expect to be chided a little if you go to working class bars. Tahitians are generally polite, but often the visitor bears the brunt of their jokes. Laugh along. One evening at a local dive, several Americans were fortunate enough to be entertained by one drunken Tahitian comedian who alternately plunked away at a ukulele and told outrageous jokes. He was bringing the house down. The routine was entirely in Tahitian, and the Americans were the butt of every joke. Probably the best bar in this category is the *Kikiri* a few blocks from Boulevard Pomare.

For the average Tahitian, the dance halls (as opposed to the discos), are the most popular places to go. All the dance halls have amplified sound systems and bands that play the same Tahitian waltzes, fox trots, rock 'n' roll and music for the sensual *tamure*, the hip-shaking dance. Of these spots the classiest and certainly the one with the prettiest vahines is *La Cave*, beneath the Royal Papeete Hotel. You could also try the *Pub Tiare*, adjacent to the Pitate on Boulevard Pomare. La Cave has more of a ballroom atmosphere than the dance halls. Virtually everyone in Tahiti dances, sings, plays guitar, or does it all. Music and dance play an extremely important role in Tahitian culture. To not take part in this is to miss a large slice of the Tahitian experience.

Continuing on the dance hall circuit, down the socio-economic ladder from La Cave is the Pitate on Boulevard Pomare, with its garish red lights and movie posters on the ceiling. The Pitate is the most popular club among working-class

Tahitians. At the door sits a bouncer with fists the size of hams. During the course of the evening couples file past him and disappear into the parking lot across the street only to return several minutes later. 'There is,' as one local put it, 'very little pretension at the Pitate.'

Discos. They seem to have a universal character − flashing lights, a pulsating beat and a high decibel level. There are three types of discos in Papeete: the seedy B-girl hangouts frequented by French sailors; those popular with transvestites (and French sailors); and the posh 'straight' discos.

The first category, located on the waterfront near the naval yard, should be avoided. The second variety, which includes the *Piano Bar* and the *Bounty Club*, have the 'loosest' ambience in town and attract a mixed crowd of tourists, locals, servicemen, gays and straights. Everyone is accepted here, and you can spend the evening dancing or watching the assorted types filter in and out through the swinging doors. The Piano Bar is a meeting place for the *mahus* (transvestites), and it features strip shows with female impersonators. When it is time for the show to begin, the music stops and patrons gather in a semicircle before the mirrored wall of the stage like school children awaiting a puppet show. With a vaudeville flair, the owner announces the entrance of Gigi, and the disc jockey cranks up Donna Summer or Michael Jackson to a deafening level. From stage left emerges Gigi, knees pumping and bottom swaying, making her way to a solitary bar stool in the middle of the dance floor.

She stands over six feet tall in her five-inch chromium-plated shoes and is wearing a skimpy leopard-skin outfit. Strands of hair from her wig fly in all directions as she bumps and grinds her way across the stage and contorts her body on the stool. Meanwhile, the audience is in rapt attention. The women giggle, the French sailors leer, and the American tourists try hard to be nonchalant. Within a few minutes into the next song, Gigi's clothing has been peeled off and a drunk Tahitian teenager is sitting near her groping for her G-string. He is harmless and nobody pays attention to him. With a casual but deft flick of the wrist, Gigi removes even the G-string and disappears backstage.

At the tables, the hum of conversation resumes. Several uniformed sailors, still covered with acne, are animatedly flirting with a mahu. Although her demeanor and husky voice mark her as a transvestite, there are other mahus who are not so obvious. Often the transvestites rival women in their beauty − an occurrence which, since the time of Cook, has led to some surprising discoveries by the unwary visitor.

Leaving the Piano Bar behind, you can try the 'straight' discos which include the *Lido, Club 106, Le Retro, The Rolls Club* and the ultra-posh *Mayana* − all places to be seen for the young and the restless. The Mayana caters to a younger, 'teenybopper' crowd while Le Retro's patrons are usually older. All the clubs are located near the waterfront or the Vaima Center area, within a few minutes' walk from each other.

On a Saturday night, a quiet cocktail can be had at *La Jonque*, a remodelled boat anchored across from the Pitate Club. Likewise the major hotels in the area like the *Beachcomber* or the *Tahara'a* provide a tranquil ambience if you are not up to the nightclubs. When the bars close down (after 2 am), the *Princess Heita* in Pirae picks up the after-hours crowd. There you can either continue drinking and dancing or head to the 'trucks' for a bite to eat.

GETTING THERE

Travellers arriving in French Polynesia by air will all arrive in Papeete. See the introductory Getting There section about flying to Tahiti. Papeete is also the central travel point for all of French Polynesia. From here flights fan out to the other islands and it is also the main port for copra boats which service the more remote islands. See the introductory Getting Around section for details of domestic flights and copra boat schedules. Or see the individual island sections for details of transport there from Tahiti.

GETTING AROUND

Short of renting a car in Tahiti, there are three other modes of transportation: 'Le Truck,' taxis and hitch-hiking.

Le Truck

The bus system, known as Le Truck, is the most practical and widely used form of transportation on the island. The trucks, which are somewhere between jitneys and buses, have wooden benches that run the length of the vehicle, no shock absorbers, and speakers that blast Tahitian music and rock 'n' roll. Each driver is an owner-operator, who, like all independent truck drivers, must hustle to survive. The trucks have a few official highway stops (with canopies and benches), but generally they will pull over along any stretch of the road if you wave them down.

The trucks run on weekdays from the first light of dawn until about 10 pm. On Saturday they operate until midnight, and Sunday is the drivers' day off. The main departure point for all trucks is the central marketplace in Papeete. To go west (towards Faaa Airport) you must catch Le Truck from Rue du 22 Sept 1914 on the west side of the market. To go east (towards Pirae), catch a truck on the opposite side of the market on Rue Cardella (see map). Drivers are always paid after the trip is completed. Fare is about 100 cfp.

Taxis

Compared to those in other locales, taxis in French Polynesia are expensive. The government regulates taxi fares and rates have been established from Papeete to virtually every hotel and restaurant. Base rate is 330 cfp and to get anywhere within

Papeete should not be over 400 cfp. Tariff from town to the airport or vice versa is 700 cfp, except after 10 pm when the price for this particular route goes up 50%. All other fares double from 10 pm to 6 am and on holidays the minimum rate may go up 25%. Daytime hourly rates are 2000 cfp or 55 cfp per km. Any complaints should be directed to OPATTI (The Visitors Bureau).

Hitch-hiking

Hitch-hiking is also possible and can be very easy for foreigners. The idea is to be as conspicuously non-French as possible. Tahitians enjoy meeting westerners.

Car Rental

For the visitor spending any appreciable time in Tahiti or the person wishing to do an around-the-island tour solo, renting a car is a necessity. Aside from the the the big names like Budget, Hertz and Avis there are smaller, good quality rentals – but consumer beware. Scrutinise the vehicle before you drive it off, lest you find nonexistent brakes or flat tyres. Depending on your choice of model, prices range from 1700 to 3800 cfp per day or 11,000 to 20,000 cfp per week. Rates are generally based on time plus distance – gas is not included. A valid driver's licence issued in your country of residence is required. Watch out for French and Tahitian motorists who may insist on passing on blind curves, tailgating and turning without signalling. Beware also of children playing on the street, pedestrians who seem oblivious to traffic, and drunks on the weekends. The agencies are at the following locations:

Andre
    Boulevard Pomare opposite naval base in Fare Ute (tel 2-94-04)
Europcar
    Boulevard Pomare (tel 2-46-l6)
Robert
    Rue Cdr Destremeau (tel 2-97-20)
Budget
    Avenue Georges Bambridge (tel 2-66-45)

Pacificar
    Rue des Ramparts (tel 2-43-64)
Hertz
    Rue Cdr Destremeau opposite sports
    stadium (tel 2-04-71)
Avis Polynesie
    Rue Charles Vienot (tel 2-96-49)

Airport Transport

Faaa Airport is six km (four miles) from
Papeete. 'Le Truck' takes 15 minutes into
town and costs 70 cfp. There are also
plenty of taxis. Taxi rates are set by the
government and are fixed from the airport
to each hotel. Taxi fare from the airport to
Papeete is 700 cfp.

Airport Facilities Facilities at Tahiti's
International Airport at Faaa include:

Two banks, open an hour before international flights depart and until an hour
after arrival.

A post office (open regular hours).
An OPATTI (Office of Tourism) information booth for arriving international
flights.
A 'consigne' (storage area for luggage) and
shower facilities for in-transit passengers.
Three duty-free shops and a (non-duty-
free) boutique, *Manureva*, which has
fashions, souvenirs and a newsstand.
Gallerie Leonard da Vinci is an art gallery.
Across from the airport is a *fare* where old
women sell purses, hats, shells, flower and
shell leis for departing friends and relatives.
A snack bar with restaurant upstairs.
Two car rental offices (Hertz and Avis).
Offices for Air New Zealand, Qantas, Lan
Chile, Polynesian Airlines and Air Polyn-
esie. In separate buildings are offices for
Tahiti Helicopter and Tahiti Conquest
Airlines, both charter carriers.

Moorea

Lying 19 km west of Tahiti is Moorea, the only other major island in the Windward group. It covers an area of 132 square km and has a population of nearly 6000. After Tahiti, it is the second most popular tourist attraction and, aside from Tahiti and Bora Bora, it is the island slated for the most tourist development over the next few years. Moorea is quick and easy to reach from Tahiti – shuttle flights leave every 20 minutes from Faaa Airport and ferry boats depart from Papeete daily.

Moorea, which means 'yellow lizard,' is a name taken from a family of chiefs which eventually united with the Pomare dynasty. The island is serrated with sharp peaks that command deep cleft valleys, once centres for vanilla cultivation. Pineapple has now replaced vanilla as the biggest cash crop. Seen from the air, Moorea is encircled by a lagoon of translucent green and is fringed by an azure sea. It has a triangular shape, one side with two large but shallow bays (Cook's Bay and Opunohu).

Archaeological evidence in the Opunohu Valley suggests that people were living on the island as early as 1600 AD, which corresponds with the oral history of the valley. At the time of Cook's arrival in 1774, there was internecine fighting among the islands' chiefs and warfare with tribes on neighbouring Tahiti. The battles continued for many years and the arrival of the missionaries in 1805 actually helped the Pomare dynasty gain power in Tahiti by supplying arms and mercenaries in return for support. After Pomare I conquered Tahiti, Moorea (which had been his refuge) became no more than a province of the Tahitian kingdom. During the latter half of the 19th century, colonists arrived and cotton and coconut plantations began to spring up. Vanilla and coffee cultivation came later, in the 20th century.

AROUND THE ISLAND

I recommend staying a few days in Moorea to get the feel of the place. The visitor will immediately note that the pace is much slower than that of Tahiti and people tend to be friendlier. The thing to do is take an around-the-island tour by renting a car or a scooter or by going with one of the organised groups advertised by every hotel.

The following guide begins at PK 0, at the airport. For ease of reference there are (as on Tahiti) km posts along the road, which start at PK 1 going in both directions from the airport. Thus there will be posts PK 1 at Temae Village (heading west) and at the Hotel Kia Ora (heading east). In this guide we will go west, in an anti-clockwise direction.

Temae Village (1 km)

It was here that novelist Herman Melville persuaded the chief to have the vahines perform the erotic 'Lory-Lory' for him; it was a dance forbidden by the missionaries. The author came here shortly after his release from jail in Tahiti where he and other crew members of the *Lucy Ann* were punished for their participation in a mutiny.

Bali Hai Hotel (4 km)

The hotel includes the Coconut House Restaurant, Chez Christian Restaurant and 'Maison Blanc.' The latter is a renovated, turn-of-the-century plantation house owned by one of the principals of the Bali Hai Hotel. With the vanilla boom during the latter part of the 19th and early 20th centuries a number of this type of home were built in Moorea, but none are in such excellent shape. With a careful eye you can still see other plantation houses tucked away in the bush or along the side of the road. Style consists of clapboard construction, roofing iron and a verandah with white wooden fretwork.

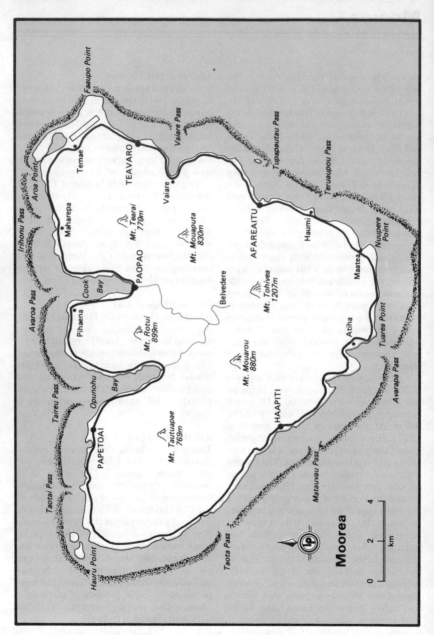

Moorea

Top: Moorea from the air (TTB)
Bottom: On the beach, Moorea (JW)

Top: Marae in Maeva, Huahine (RK)
Left: Dr Sinoto, expert on eastern Polynesia, excavating an ancient canoe bailer on the grounds of the Bali Hai Hotel in Huahine (RK)
Right: More finds from same excavation, note fishhook in the centre (RK)

Moorea Supermarket & Bank of Indo Suez (5 km)

Entrance to Cook's Bay (7 km)
This is the modern-day location of Galerie van der Heyde, a fine art shop. The bay was also one of the sites for the recent production of *Return of the Bounty*.

Bali Hai Club (8 km)
The Bali Hai Club (formerly the Aimeo Hotel) is also the site for a Bank of Tahiti branch, Chez Albert, Hakka Restaurant, a gas station, Aimeo Boutique and the Teva Black Pearl Boutique.

Pao Pao Village (9 km)
This village is the site of the main dock used by trading vessels and has a pharmacy, Chinese stores, school, infirmary, Bank of Polynesie, doctor's office and the turnoff for the Belvedere vista point and Opunohu Valley marae. The doctor's phone number is 6-10-04.

Catholic Church (10 km)
This Catholic church has an altar inlaid with mother-of-pearl.

Pineapple Cannery (11 km)

Robinson's Cove (17 km)
A popular yacht anchorage.

Opunohu Valley Entrance (18 km)
This is the second entrance to the Opunohu Valley road linking up with Pao Pao, the valley's marae and the Belvedere vista. Just prior to the road junction are prawn ponds.

Papetoai (21 km)
Papetoai was formerly the seat of the Pomare I government and the scene of his conversion to Christianity. An octagonal church built by the London Missionary Society still stands here – it is the oldest European building in use in the South Pacific. (In 1811, years before Moorea's importance as a vanilla-growing region, the island was the London Missionary Society's centre for evangelical work for the entire Pacific.) In the back of the churchyard is a solar energy panel. Also in the area are Chinese stores, a post office and a school.

Les Tipanier Hotel/Restaurant (25 km)
Excellent restaurant and moderately priced accommodation.

Club Med, Campground, Escargot Restaurant (26 km)

End of Black-topped Road (28 km)
Here the 'sauvage' side of Moorea emerges, with fewer people and a foretaste of life on the outer islands of French Polynesia. There are scattered copra plantations and the feeling is more rural. At this point there is a gap in the km posts and the next marker is PK 24.

Haapiti Village (24 km)
The village has a soccer field, Chinese store and Catholic church.

Atiha Bay (20 km)
Pirogues (canoes) are set on blocks along the side of the road and nets hang from poles or ironwood trees.

Maatea Village (14 km)
There is a Chinese store, school and movie house.

Haumi Village (12 km)

Afareatiu Village (10 km)
Located here are Moorea's administrative centre, shops, a church, Hotel Pauline, a school and a road to an interior waterfall. Afareatiu, Papetoai, Haapiti and Maharepa were all communities built around ancient temples and chiefs' dwellings of former times.

Vaiare Bay (5 km)
Here you will find the dock for cargo boats and the passenger cruiser *Keke III*, which

sails daily from Papeete. If you have the opportunity, watch the loading and unloading of passengers and cargo at the dock.

Kia Ora Hotel (1 km) The hotel offers the most luxurious accommodation on the island.

Bali Hai Story

It is impossible to write about tourism on Moorea without mentioning the Bali Hai Boys: Jay Carlisle, Muk McCallum and Hugh Kelly. After arriving in Moorea in 1961, the three invested in a run-down vanilla plantation and inadvertently became owners of a ramshackle hotel. Their timing was impeccable. Airlines were just beginning to land in Tahiti, and when a journalist discovered their dumpy but charming hotel, success was just around the next coconut tree. Since then, the 'boys' have established hotels on Raiatea and Huahine, and have turned the original plantation into a successful experimental farm and egg-laying facility. The Bali Hai Boys are reputed to be hard workers, generous employers and freespending good-timers.

Lumbering Hugh Kelly is fond of telling the story of the return of Moorea's missing *tikis*. The two stone reliefs were located in an ancient religious shrine on the vanilla plantation and were left undisturbed by the three Americans. A week after Kelly showed them to a wealthy Honolulu businessman, the tikis disappeared. Kelly denied rumours that he had sold the priceless artifacts and vowed to somehow get them back. Several years passed with no trace of the relics, until an American woman approached Kelly with some startling news. She had seen the tikis at the Honolulu home of the same businessman who was the last person to see them in Moorea. Apparently this man was an avid collector of Polynesian artifacts.

Hugh Kelly decided to take the matter into his own hands. He flew to Honolulu and questioned the teenaged son of the businessman about the tikis. The son insisted he knew nothing until Kelly blurted out a tear-jerking tale of a dying Tahitian woman who supposedly owned the tikis. With mock anguish, Kelly claimed the woman was shivering on her deathbed because she thought the tikis were in a cold place. The boy broke down and assured Kelly the tikis were in a warm place – on the balcony of his father's apartment. That was all the wily Kelly had to know. He confronted the businessman and threatened to spread the word to the Honolulu papers if the man didn't return the tikis. Faced with an embarrassing situation, the businessman consented. Several months later, amid pomp, press coverage from Tahiti and Hawaii, and incantations by Moorea's *tahua* (shaman), the sacred tikis were returned intact to their age-old shrine.

OPUNOHU VALLEY

The Opunohu Valley, with its reconstructed *marae* (temples), excellent vista and lush meadows, is well worth the detour off the perimeter road. In the precontact era this valley was teeming with people but is now largely deserted and devoted to agriculture. Its population declined in the early 19th century, soon after the abandonment of the traditional religion.

Over 500 ancient structures have been recorded here, including religious and secular stone buildings and agricultural terraces. The complexity of the remains indicates a highly developed social system. The chief remnants of these buildings are six marae, reconstructed by Y H Sinoto of the Bishop Museum in Honolulu in 1967. A council platform and two archery platforms have also been rebuilt. From the junction at Pao Pao (nine km) it is several winding km to the marae. All are an easy walk from the road.

Marae Ahu-o-Mahine

This marae has the most elaborate form and features a three-stepped *ahu* (platform). It was once the community marae for the Opunohu Valley and was built some time after 1780 AD. Note that it is constructed with hand-crafted, round dressed stones, similar to those of Marae Arahurahura in Paea, Tahiti.

Archery Platforms

Archery was a sacred sport in ancient Tahiti, practised only by people of high rank – chiefs' families and warriors. As is clearly visible from the map, archery

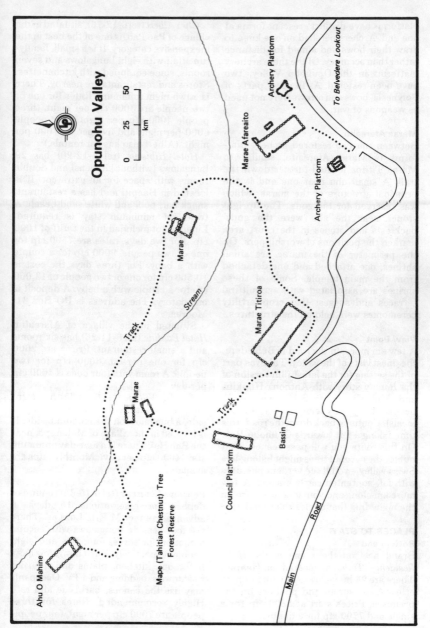

Opunohu Valley

To Belvedere Lookout

Archery Platform

Marae Afareaito

Archery Platform

Marae Titiroa

Marae

Stream

Track

Track

Marae

Council Platform

Bassin

Main Road

Mape (Tahitian Chestnut) Tree Forest Reserve

Ahu O Mahine

0   25   50
km

platforms have distinct crescent forms at one end. Archers perched on one knee to draw their bows and aimed for distance rather than accuracy. Of the three archery platforms in the Opunohu Valley, two have been restored. As in other parts of Polynesia, bows and arrows were not used as weapons of war.

Marae Afareaito

Between the two restored archery platforms is Marae Afareaito, similar to Marae Titiroa located further down the trail. A small ahu near one end is the principal structure of the marae, which was reserved for the gods. The upright stones near the ahu were the gods' backrests and stones in the court area marked the positions of worshippers. On the perimeter of the marae are small shrines, one attached and one detached from the main temple. Some of these shrines are associated with agricultural terraces and suggest that crop-fertility ceremonies were held on the structures.

View Point

A few km more up the road is Belvedere, the finest vista of the valley. This was part of the setting for the latest film version of the Bounty story with Anthony Hopkins and Mel Gibson (which gave much-needed temporary employment to the locals). Continue back down the road, this time taking a left towards Opunohu Bay. On this route you will pass scenery that but for the coconut trees might belong to a Swiss valley – you'll see verdant pastures with fat, contented cattle grazing. A few more km along and you are once more on the main drag that circles the island.

PLACES TO STAY
Bottom end

Brand new on the scene is the *Hotel Residence Tiahura*, located in Haapiti. There are 24 bungalows, 18 with kitchenettes. A restaurant and pool are on the premises. Prices start at 5800 cfp for a single and 7700 cfp for a double.

Chez Albert (tel 6-12-76), situated in the village of Pao Pao, is one of the best in the inexpensive category. It is a small, family-run affair with eight bungalows and seven rooms, some equipped with kitchenettes. Stores and restaurants are nearby. There is a two-night minimum. Rates for one or two people are 3000 cfp per night, three people 4000 cfp per night, four people 6000 cfp per night and five people 7000 cfp per night. (Albert also has car rentals.)

Hotel Hibiscus (tel 6-12-20) has 29 bungalows (without kitchens) and double rooms with space for an extra cot. It is located in Haapiti and has a restaurant, snack bar, pool and white sand beach. A two-night minimum stay is required. Linen is not included in the tariff of 1000 cfp. For two days, rates are 7500 cfp for one or two people, 9000 cfp for a couple with a baby. For three days the cost is 10,500 cfp for one or two people or 13,000 cfp for a couple with a baby. A deposit is mandatory. The address is PO Box 31, Moorea.

Situated in the village of Afareatiu, *Hotel Pauline* (tel 6-11-26) has six rooms and a small restaurant. Prices are 2000 cfp for one person, 3000 cfp for two people. A room with four beds is 4000 cfp per day.

Tia Tia Village (tel 6-10-35) has eight bungalows with kitchens on the ocean side, a bungalow on the mountain side. It is located in the village of Maharepa, near the Bali Hai. There is a four-day minimum stay (4000 cfp per day). Monthly rates are available.

Pensions *Linareva* (tel 6-15-35) requires a deposit for reservations 15 days in advance; contact M Eric Lussiez. There are four seaside bungalows with accommodation for three, four, five and eight people respectively. Each bungalow has a bathroom, kitchen, plates and utensils, washtowels, bedding and a TV. Occupants may use the canoes, barbecue and raft. Highly recommended. Rates for three people are 7000 cfp per night, four people

9000 cfp per night, five people 11,000 cfp per night and eight people 16,000 cfp per night. The address is PO Box 205, Temae, Moorea.

Near the Bali Hai in Maharepa is *Chez Mama Loulou* (tel 6-10-71) with two bungalows without kitchen and a communal bathroom. Rates are 2400 cfp per day (one or two people).

Chez Samuel Russel (tel 6-13-23) in Pihaena has three rooms with a common bathroom. Guests may use the kitchen. Rates are 2500 cfp per day (one or two people).

Chez Nicole (tel 6-15-66) in Haapiti has four rooms with a common bathroom and use of the kitchen. There is also a seaside bungalow. Bicycles and a canoe are available. Double, triple and quadruple accommodation is available for 3500, 4500 and 5500 cfp per day respectively. The mailing address is PO Box 6619, Faaa, Tahiti.

Camping This is one of only two 'official' campgrounds I heard about in French Polynesia. It is located next to Club Med and is run by a woman named Anna. Bus service is available from the campground to the dock. Spartan amenities; cost is 300 cfp per night.

Middle

Climat Moorea (tel 6-15-48) is a newly constructed 40-room, 46-bungalow hotel located near the Club Med on the beach. It has a restaurant, a bar, windsurfing, snorkelling, a swimming pool and tennis. Tariffs begin at 7300 cfp for a single and 9500 cfp for a double. The address is Haapiti, Moorea.

An excellent, moderately priced hotel/restaurant/ bar is *Les Tipaniers* (tel 6-12-67), run by a very nice Italian woman who doubles as a fine chef. The hotel is located near Club Med. Some of the 21 units are equipped with kitchenettes. There are free outrigger canoes and excursions. This place deserves an A-1 recommendation. Prices are 6900 cfp for a single and 9200 cfp for a double. Write PO Box 1002, Moorea.

Club Mediterranee Moorea (tel 2-96-99), recently refurbished, is one of the originals, and like all Club Meds is a focal point for the young, the hip and the restless. With planned activities, it is a sort of summer camp for adults located on a gorgeous lagoon with many *motus* (islets) to explore. Rates are US$700 per week per person (includes room, three meals and all sporting activities). The address is PO Box 575, Papeete.

Captain Cook Beach Hotel (tel 6-10-60) near Club Med has 12 brand-new units and a pool – the latest additions to this facility of 20 bungalows and 36 rooms. It offers all water sport activities, canoes, cycling, tennis, stables and snorkelling. Prices begin at 10,700 cfp for a single and 11,700 cfp for a double. The address is Haapiti, Moorea.

New Kaveka (tel 6-10-50) is located on Cook's Bay. It has 22 bungalows, water sports (including scuba diving), a white sand beach and a bar/restaurant. Rates are 8900 cfp for a single or double. Write PO Box 13, Moorea.

Located just down the road from Captain Cook is *Moorea Village* (tel 6-10-02). It has 50 Tahitian-style bungalows, (15 with kitchenettes), a pool, bar, restaurant, tennis and volleyball facilities and a beach. Prices begin at 5000 cfp for a single and 6000 cfp for a double. The address is Haapiti, Moorea.

On the beach about four km from the village of Pao Pao is *Moorea Lagoon* (tel 6-14-68 or 6-11-55). The atmosphere is friendly and very Tahitian; approximately half of the clientele is local. There are 45 rooms and four bungalows, suites with a jacuzzi, five hectares of gardens, a pool, bicycles, a bar/restaurant, a boutique and conference facilities. You can take advantage of a full array of water sports including an 'Aqua 6' – a sort of surface submarine used for viewing underwater life without getting wet. There's also a fire dancing show every Saturday night. Rates

begin at 8500 cfp for a single and 9500 cfp for a double. Write PO Box 11, Moorea.

Top end

Located at the entrance of Cook's Bay and close to the air strip, the *Bali Hai Moorea* (tel 6-13-59) is a well-run hotel established by the now legendary Bali Hai Boys – three Americans who came before the Tahiti tourist boom to run a vanilla plantation and wound up hotel magnates. The hotel has a good restaurant, two bars, a white sand beach, water sports, Liki Tiki cruises, tennis, pool and a breathtakingly beautiful setting. There are 63 units. Prices start at 12,600 cfp for a single and 14,700 cfp for a double. Write PO Box 415, Papeete. In addition to the Bali Hai Moorea there is now a second location, *Club Bali Hai* on Cook's Bay, which operates a time-sharing programme and also rents rooms that start at 8400 cfp for a single and 10,500 cfp for a double.

Situated on a white sand beach facing Tahiti, the *Kia Ora Moorea* (tel 2-86-72) is the most luxurious and perhaps the most beautiful of the hotels on Moorea. It has a disco aboard an old, converted inter-island schooner just offshore and 66 newly built units. There are three bars, two restaurants (one of them an exceptional gourmet restaurant) and all the amenities you could want such as a boutique, car rental, outrigger canoes, tennis, wind-surfing, sailboats and scuba diving. Prices for singles or doubles begin at 13,800 cfp. The address is PO Box 706, Papeete.

PLACES TO EAT

It is hard to go wrong at any restaurant in French Polynesia. Prices for Moorea's restaurants listed here don't include wine.

Escargot (near Club Med). French cuisine and seafood, 1000-2000 cfp, recommended.
Coconut House (near Bali Hai). Local Tahitian and French cuisine, 800-2000 cfp, recommended.
Hakka Restaurant (Cook's Bay). Chinese, 1500-2000 cfp.
Manava Restaurant (Cook's Bay). Chinese and Tahitian food, 800-1300 cfp.

Chez Christian (near Bali Hai). French and local cuisine, 1000-1200 cfp.

Tipanier (near Club Med). Italian and French specialities, 800-2000 cfp, recommended.

ENTERTAINMENT

There isn't much nightlife except at *Pim's Club*, the swinging *Club Med* and the *Kia Ora Hotel's* disco. The former is mainly young and Tahitian in ambience – packed, full of drunk kids and punctuated by an innocuous fist fight or two. If you are in the proper mood, it can be a lot of fun. The Club Med, which has nightly entertainment, can also be an interesting hangout. However, if you are not staying there you must buy a quantity of beads in order to purchase drinks – they do not accept cash. The Kia Ora disco – located on an old, converted inter-island steamer – is elegant and urbane. All the 'right' people come here to dance the night away. Drinks are expensive, the young girls look like models out of *Vogue* and there are definitely more Europeans around than at Pim's.

GETTING THERE
Air

Air Polynesie flights depart every 20 minutes or so from Faaa Airport, and Air Tahiti flights are also regularly scheduled. There are also regular flights between Moorea and Bora Bora, Huahine, Manihi, Maupiti, Raiatea and Rangiroa. See the introductory Getting Around section for more information on air fares.

Sea

There are several boats you can take from Papeete. They are docked on the quay several hundred metres up Boulevard Pomare from the tourism office, Fare Manihini (where the 'trucks' or food vendors park at night). The swiftest and newest among these is the *Keke III*, a sleek cruiser that makes up to 20 knots and can carry up to 200 passengers. It is air conditioned and has a bar. On the cruise over keep an eye open for flying fish propelling themselves off the crests of the waves and dolphins swimming up to the bow. There is also the old-style (and slower) ferry, the *Maire II*, crammed to the scuppers with men, women, children, animals, cars, cases of Hinano beer and every other provision imaginable. It also operates daily from Papeete.

The daily schedule for the *Keke III* is as follows:

7.00 am	Papeete-Vaiare	35 mins
9.15 am	Papeete-Cook's Bay	55 mins
2.30 pm	Papeete-Vaiare	35 mins
8.00 am	Vaiare-Papeete	35 mins
4.00 pm	Cook's Bay-Papeete	55 mins
6.30 pm	Vaiare-Papeete	35 mins

Upon landing at either Cook's Bay or Vaiare (the administrative centre), buses (Le Truck) or taxis are available to other parts of the island. One-way fares are 750 cfp to Vaiare and 900 cfp to Cook's Bay.

GETTING AROUND

As on most of the outer islands, the larger hotels will supply guests with bicycles and can arrange car rentals. Independent rental agencies on the island include Billy's Rent-A-Car near the Club Med, Moorea Rent-A-Car (next door to Billy's which has motor bikes as well), Paopao Rent-A-Car at Cook's Bay (which has cars and scooters) and Albert's Rentals next to them, which also has cars and scooters. It is difficult to see Moorea without a motorised vehicle (or a guided tour) so you may well find yourself in the position of renting something. Be sure and check your car or scooter for minor details like inflated tyres and brakes that work.

Huahine

Huahine, 176 km north-west of Papeete, has a population of approximately 4000. It is actually two islands, Huahine-Iti and Huahine-Nui (Little Huahine and Big Huahine) which are part of the same land mass and are connected at low tide by an isthmus. (For the convenience of motorists, there is a bridge.) The island is verdant and rugged and along the coastline are several gorgeous bays.

The residents have a long tradition of fierce pride and independence. According to a Tahitian proverb, 'Obstinacy is their diversion.' To this day, their cockiness is intact and their practical jokes may be a memorable part of the visitor's experience.

Huahine is also a landmark for surfers. Although it does not have the kind of waves that will bring people flocking from Hawaii or Australia, it does have the best surfing in French Polynesia.

Pouvanaa

Huahine is the birthplace of Pouvanaa a Oopa, the greatest contemporary French Polynesian leader. Pouvanaa, a decorated WW I veteran, was the son of a Danish sailor and a Polynesian woman. In 1947 he was jailed by the French for advocating Polynesian veterans' rights, and became the spokesperson for the Tahitian Independence Movement. Blessed with charismatic oratorical skills and well versed in the Bible, Pouvanaa established himself as the most powerful politician in the French Polynesian Territorial Assembly. Known as 'Metua' – 'beloved father to the Tahitians,' he lambasted the colonial system for its treatment of Polynesians as second-class citizens and fought for legislative reforms that would grant Polynesians greater autonomy.

At the zenith of his power, Pouvanaa was convicted of conspiracy in a plot to burn down Papeete and was sent to the notorious Baumette prison in Marseilles. At age 64 he was sentenced to eight years of solitary confinement and banished from Polynesia for another 15 years. Ten years later he was pardoned for the crime many felt he did not commit and returned to Tahiti. Eventually he went back into politics and again served in the Territorial Assembly. He died in 1976. For an excellent account of Pouvanaa's life, Bengt Danielsson's *Moruroa Mon Amour* is recommended. (See bibliography.)

FARE

The small community of Fare, which faces the waterfront, is the island's main settlement and has the usual Chinese shops, a quay to accommodate the copra boats and several pension-style hotels. Fare is almost 'Wild West' in character with its one main street shaded by huge trees and its old-fashioned clapboard stores. It is a slow-moving town in the heat of the day – an occasional auto may pass and kick up some dust or the air may be disturbed by the sounds of school children giggling or bicycle tyres gliding across the road. Several buses provide transportation to such far-flung communities as Parea on the opposite end of the island or the village of Maeva, a 10-minute ride from Fare. Roads are excellent and follow the often steep contours of the terrain, making it worthwhile renting a car for an around-the-island trip.

MAEVA

In ancient times Huahine was a centre of Polynesian culture and was ruled by a centralised government instead of by warring tribes as most of the islands were. Archaeologically, Huahine is the richest island in French Polynesia and is sometimes referred to as an 'open-air museum.' In the village of Maeva alone are 16 restored marae, the ancestral shrines of local chiefs. The stone slabs of these ancient temples jut out like phalluses on the landscape and are eerily reminiscent

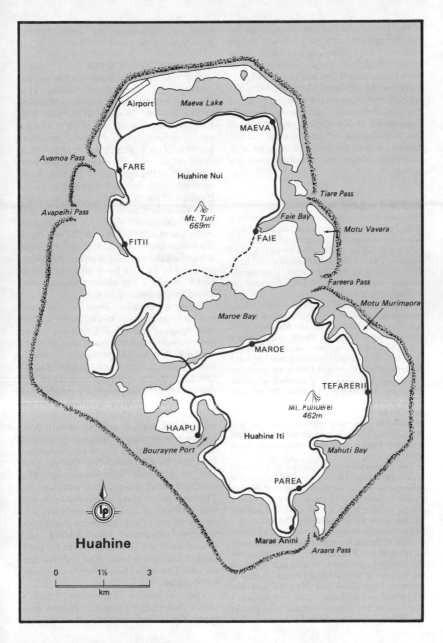

Airport
Maeva Lake
MAEVA
Avamoa Pass
FARE
Huahine Nui
Tiare Pass
Avapeihi Pass
Mt. Turi
669m
Faie Bay
FITII
FAIE
Motu Vavara
Fareera Pass
Motu Murimaora
Maroe Bay
MAROE
TEFARERII
Mt. Puhuerei
462m
HAAPU
Huahine Iti
Bourayne Port
Mahuti Bay
PAREA
Marae Anini
Araara Pass

Huahine

0   1½   3
km

of the Druid ruins of Stonehenge. In the nearby lagoon, rich in crab and other seafood, are nine ancient fish traps constructed from stone, some of which have been rebuilt and are in use today.

Above the village on Matairea Hill is the second most important temple in all of French Polynesia and more recently discovered archaeological sites, such as the foundations of priests' and chiefs' homes, more temples and a huge wall guarding the mountain sanctuary from sea raiders.

Mystery of Matairea Hill

The coastal flats of Maeva – where the majority of the reconstructed temples are located – was, according to royal tradition, subdivided by the eight royal families of Huahine for purposes of worship. That all the royal families would have their temples in the same area is extremely unusual and suggests a large number of retainers living nearby.

According to tradition, the second most important temple in French Polynesia, marae Matairea-rahi, is located on Matairea Hill above Maeva. Dr Y H Sinoto (the world's authority on Eastern Polynesian archaeology) of Honolulu's Bishop Museum, familiar with the temple ruins, surveyed the area and upon noting the presence of a number of stone structures assumed he had found the remains of the retainers' homes. Upon further investigation, however, instead of retainers' residences he found 40 previously unrecorded marae and realised the area was a much more important religious centre than had previously been thought.

The excavations on Matairea Hill proved significant because they uncovered for the first time marae of the Leeward group that were of similar construction to those of the Windward group. Although the Windward and Leeward islands were allied politically and culturally, marae found in both groups had always been of greatly different construction – an archaeological mystery. The discovery of the Matairea Hill temples provided a 'missing link' between the cultures of the Leeward Islands (Huahine, Raiatea, Bora Bora and Maupiti) and the Windward group (Tahiti, Maio and Moorea.) The excavations indicate that marae located in the Windward group probably originated in Huahine, reinforcing the early cultural importance of the island.

ARCHAEOLOGICAL SITES

Along with the very many visible marae, underground excavations reveal that Huahine has the oldest known settlement in the Society Islands. The Vaito'otia/Fa'ahia site came to light in 1972 when a war club (similar in design to artifacts found in New Zealand) was dragged from the bottom of a pond during the construction of the Bali Hai Hotel near Fare. Archaeologist Sinoto happened to be on Huahine at the time of the club's discovery and was called to the scene. Realising it was a significant find, he coordinated subsequent excavation with the owners of the hotel. Between 1973-1981 Dr Sinoto unearthed the remains of an entire village, believed to be have been settled between 650-850 AD – the oldest remains ever found in the Society Islands.

From toolmaking areas at the site, workers unearthed habitations, canoe-making areas and a chief's house as well as numerous wooden, stone and shell artifacts – adzes, fish hooks, pendants, scrapers, canoe bailers and canoe parts. Sinoto theorises that around the year 1100 AD this particular village – whose inhabitants most likely came from the Marquesas (as indicated by the style of the artifacts) – were faced with a natural catastrophe. Either a hurricane or tsunami destroyed the village, creating a sort of Polynesian Pompeii. In all probability the villagers had to evacuate their homes quickly, leaving behind most of their possessions. This was unfortunate for the residents but was a stroke of luck for future archaeologists. Many of the otherwise perishable wooden materials were buried and preserved in the mud – literally in the back yard of the future hotel. The Bali Hai has its own fine collection of artifacts in the hotel lobby.

The excavation buttresses Sinoto's theory that early Polynesian settlers came from the Marquesas to the Society

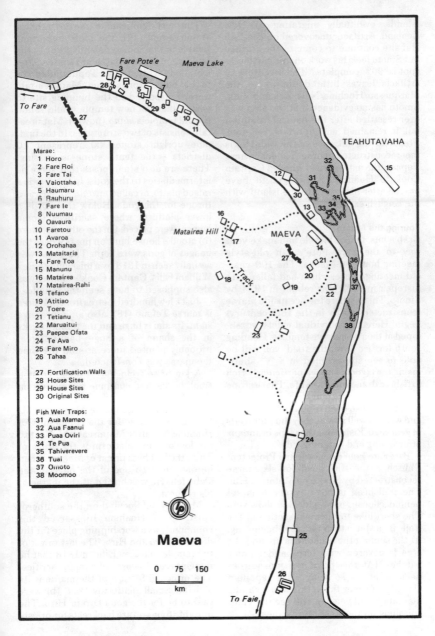

Marae:
1 Horo
2 Fare Roi
3 Fare Tai
4 Vaiottaha
5 Haumaru
6 Rauhuru
7 Fare Ie
8 Nuumau
9 Oavaura
10 Faretou
11 Avaroa
12 Orohahaa
13 Mataitaria
14 Fare Toa
15 Manunu
16 Matairea
17 Matairea-Rahi
18 Tefano
19 Atitiao
20 Toere
21 Tetianu
22 Maruaitui
23 Paepae Ofata
24 Te Ava
25 Fare Miro
26 Tahaa

27 Fortification Walls
28 House Sites
29 House Sites
30 Original Sites

Fish Weir Traps:
31 Aua Mamao
32 Aua Faanui
33 Puaa Oviri
34 Te Pua
35 Tahiverevere
36 Tuai
37 Omoto
38 Moomoo

Fare Pote'e   Maeva Lake

To Fare

TEAHUTAVAHA

Matairea Hill   MAEVA

Track

Maeva

0   75   150
km

To Faie

Islands, eventually migrating to New Zealand. Artifacts uncovered on the Bali Hai site continue to come to the surface but Sinoto feels his work on this particular spot is '90% complete.' The inventory of artifacts leaves little doubt as to the Marquesan/Huahine/New Zealand link. Sinoto has no evidence that the area was ever resettled after the natural calamity, but it remained an important religious site. Near the entrance of the Bali Hai is the reconstructed marae Tahuea where Tapaea, the native priest who led Captain Cook to Huahine, is thought to have prayed after his return to the island with the English explorer.

Touring the Marae

Grab a bus, taxi or bicycle and make your way to the Fare Pote'e, an old-style meeting house in Maeva. The 100-year-old meeting house, which had fallen into disrepair in 1972, was rebuilt in 1974 by Sinoto. This is where the oceanside marae (constructed mostly in the 16th century) begin. Here the individual chiefs worshipped at their respective temples. Heading south further down the road, you will be able to see stones piled in a 'V' shape inside the lagoon, an area particularly rich in fish, crab and other sea life. These stone structures are ancient fish weir traps, which have also been rebuilt by Dr Sinoto and work as well now as they did hundreds of years ago. Fish enter the traps by means of incoming and outgoing tides.

Past Fare Pote'e opposite the Protestant Church is the trail head for six marae reconstructed by Sinoto on Matairea Hill. The trail head is not obvious; it is set behind a house so ask a local to show you. The short hike to the main section of the trail is a bit steep at the beginning. At the summit the trail opens up, and the area is covered with ferns and manioc patches. (At this point the mosquitoes begin to attack so bring some repellent along.) In former times this was a vanilla plantation and you can still see the vines spiralling up the trees and bushes.

The most significant marae on the hill is Matairea-rahi (17), the most important temple in the Society Islands prior to the building of Taputaputea in Raiatea. Oral tradition says that when Taputaputea was to be built, stones from Matairea-rahi were transported to the building site to ensure that the new temple would retain the old temple's *mana* (power). Matairea-rahi consists of two structures: In the first, nine upright stones (a) represent 10 districts – the tenth stone is missing. There are also stone posts that serve as intermediaries to the gods. In the rear is a raised platform called an *ahu*, which was a throne for the gods. Below the ahu is a lower platform where sacrifices (some human) were placed. On the other structure (b) stood a house built on posts where the images of gods were kept. The house was actually seen in 1818 by a missionary, Rev William Ellis. Captain Cook's painter was also supposed to have seen the temple.

Just a few hundred metres from Matairea is marae Tefano (18), also an impressive sight. Its ahu is huge and the temple basks in the shade of a huge banyan tree, probably planted there around the time the marae was constructed.

A km or so from Fare Pote'e, cross a small bridge and continue to your left on the *motu* (small island) to another very impressive temple, marae Manunu. This became the marae for the community of Huahine Nui after Matairea-rahi. Next to the low offering platform is the grave of Taiti, the last high priest of Maeva. When he died in 1915 one of the huge marae slabs fell. He was buried at the marae at his request.

Marae Anini, located on the southernmost tip of Huahine Iti, served this community as a worshipping place for the deities of Oro and Hiro. The last priest of the temple told Rev Ellis in 1818 that he remembered 14 cases of human sacrifice. The principal feature of the marae is its ahu (a). Small platforms, 'ro'i' (b) were said to be for the gods Oro or Hiro. The upright stones (c) are backrests for priests and chiefs, or memorials for deceased chiefs. A small marae (d) was built when a royal family adopted a child of lower rank. A platform (e) far out on the court was where the house of Oro stood. Under each post of the house a human sacrifice was rendered.

A thorough tour of the marae near Maeva will take several hours and a bit of walking so it is suggested you do it in the early morning or late afternoon.

The archaeological complex is the core of a planned historical/ecological 'living' museum to be organised by Dr Sinoto and the French Polynesian government. Eventually, with the cooperation of the local population, scientists and the local government hope to create a master plan that will ensure the integrity and maintenance of the archaeological treasures. Ideally, Sinoto feels that agriculture can be revived by practising age-old Polynesian ecology (such as taboos against overfishing, etc) and combining it with modern agricultural and aquacultural techniques. Sinoto would also like to rebuild the chiefs' and priests' houses near the marae and have families and caretakers occupy them on a full-time basis. The master plan would in addition provide zoning recommendations as to where restaurants, hotels and commercial buildings should be built in the archaeological zone.

PLACES TO STAY
Bottom end

Hotel Bellvue (tel 6-82-76) has bungalows available and is located in the Maroe district eight km from the airport. It is on a bluff overlooking a gorgeous bay. The hotel is not fancy but it does have all the amenities including restaurant, bar, steam bath (!), horseback riding and fishing. Deposit for one night is required. Room rates (without meals) are 3000, 3500 and 4000 cfp per night for one, two and three people respectively. Bungalow rates are 6000, 7000 and 8000 cfp per night for one, two and three people respectively.

Hotel Huahine (tel 6-82-69) in Fare has 11 rooms, a restaurant and a bar. It is clean and simple; each room has an individual toilet and shower. Deposit for one night is required. Prices (with meals) are 5000 cfp per person per night, otherwise 1700 cfp per night (single), 2500 cfp per night (double) and 3500 cfp per night (triple). Lunch or dinner is approximately 2000 cfp; you must inform the proprietor if you plan to eat there. Excursions and transportation to the airport are available.

Pensions Known for its fine cooking, *Pension Enite* (tel 6-22-37) is often full to capacity. It is in Fare and has six rooms and a common bathroom. A two-day minimum stay is required. Cost is 5000 cfp per person per night, including three meals. Meals, 2000-2600 cfp, can also be ordered by non-clients but must be reserved.

Chez Lovina (tel 6-81-90) has seven rooms, each with individual toilet and shower, and two bungalows, one with occupancy for four people, the other with occupancy for eight. It is located in Fare. Rates are 2000 cfp per night for a single and 3000 cfp per night for a double. A deposit of 5000 cfp is necessary for bungalow rentals. Two canoes are available for clients.

Chez Line Ah Foussan (tel 6-82-79) has five rooms with private bathrooms. Tariff is 2000 cfp per day for one or two people.

Located in the village of Parea 28 km from the airport, *Chez Amelie Temeharo* has five rooms and a common bathroom. A 4000 cfp deposit is required and there's a two-day minimum stay, 4000 cfp per person per day including meals. Transportation to the airport is available.

Pension Meme (tel 2-61-56) in Parea has four rooms, common bathroom. Deposit is 3500 cfp, cost is 4000 cfp per person per day including meals. Traditional Tahitian feasts on Sundays and excursions to nearby islets are available. Transportation to the airport is on request.

Top end

Another slick, well-run Bali Hai operation, the *Bali Hai Huahine* (tel 6-13-59) is the most luxurious on the island. It features the usual hotel fare: dining room, two bars, pool, snorkelling, canoes, windsurfing, bicycles, cruises, tennis, white sand beach and beautifully manicured garden. There is a historical, reconstructed temple on the premises; the hotel is located on the site of the oldest discovered habitation in the Society Islands. Artifacts on display in the lobby were recovered during construction and subsequent archaeological excavation.

The Bali Hai is within walking distance of Fare, the main village on Huahine, and a 15-minute bicycle ride from the village of Maeva, site of many reconstructed temples. Write PO Box 415, Papeete. Rates begin at 11,200 cfp per day for a single and 13,300 cfp for a double.

PLACES TO EAT

Food is available at all of the hotels. The *Bali Hai* has the classiest cuisine and is the most expensive. There is only one restaurant on the island not attached to a hotel, *Snack Temarara* in Fare. It is a cosy cafe/bar set directly on the water and features seafood dishes (including lobster), steak and hamburgers. The food is reasonably priced (350-2000 cfp) and the mix of tourists and locals provides an interesting ambience. The nearby cuisine at *Enite* is also worth checking out, but reservations are necessary.

GETTING THERE

There are air connections between Huahine and Tahiti, Bora Bora, Raiatea and Maupiti. The *Temehani II* and the *Taporo IV* both operate through Huahine. See the introductory Getting Around section for more details.

GETTING AROUND

Kake Rent-a-Car (tel 6-82-59) is adjacent to the Bali Hai. Prices range from 6000-7000 cfp per day and 4000-5000 cfp per half-day, depending on the vehicle. Kake also has scooters and small Hondas available from 2500-3500 cfp per day.

Budget (tel 6-81-47) is located in Fare and has vehicles for 6000 cfp per day or 4000 cfp per half day.

Dede, in Fare, has Hondas available for 2500 cfp per day and 1500 cfp per half day.

Note that gas for your rentals can be purchased at the Faremiti or Mobil stations in Fare.

Horseback Riding

Le Petite Ferme stable (tel 6-82-98), located halfway between the airport and Fare, has 10 horses and an able 'wrangler,' Yves Montout. M Montout takes group camping tours of two days or more as well as shorter rides. Cost is 2000 cfp for two hours, 3000 cfp for four hours, 5000 cfp for day rides including a picnic.

Raiatea & Tahaa

Forty km (25 miles) west of Huahine are the sister islands of Raiatea and Tahaa. The two share a common lagoon.

RAIATEA

Raiatea is the largest of the Leeward Islands (with an area of 170 square km) and has about 6500 inhabitants. The island is totally surrounded by a reef but has several navigable passes and the only navigable river (the Faaroa) in French Polynesia. Raiatea receives plenty of rainfall to irrigate its fertile soil and has a lagoon rich in sea life. Its main products are copra and vanilla. Scientists are also developing oyster breeding in the town of Uturoa.

Like Huahine, Raiatea is an archaeologist's delight. Scientists have unearthed artifacts linking the island with Hawaii, which corresponds with local tradition that says Raiatea was the great jumping-off point for ancient Polynesian mariners. There are also a significant number of marae, including Taputaputea, considered the most important temple in the Society Islands and a national monument. The tumbled-down ruins of the great temple are located just past the village of Opoa, about 35 km from Uturoa.

Omai

Raiatea is the home of Omai, the first Polynesian to visit Europe. When Captain Cook arrived in the Society Islands on his second voyage in 1773, Omai expressed a fervent desire to see 'Britannia.' His wish was granted and he soon became the darling of English society. Although a simpleton, Omai was friendly and charming. Dressed by his benefactors in velvet jackets, he dined in London's best homes, met the king, learned to shoot and skate, and became a favourite with the ladies.

En route back to Tahiti, he served Captain Cook as a translator in the Society Islands and Tonga. He returned to Tahiti in 1776 bearing gifts of firearms, wine, tin soldiers, kitchenware and a globe of the world. The hapless Omai was cheated out of many of his treasures by Tahitians, so Cook saw to it that he was moved to Huahine. Cook's carpenters built Omai a house there and supplied him with pigs, chickens and tools. Omai bid farewell to the crew, who had become his close friends, and held back his tears until it came time to say goodbye to Cook.

Mt Temehani

The highest point on the island is Mt Temehani (1033 metres), which can be climbed. According to tradition one of the principal Polynesian gods, Oro, was born of this volcano. Temehani is also the home of the *tiare apetahi*, a white flower found only on this mountain. Legend has it that the blossom's five petals represent the five fingers of a young Tahitian maiden who fell in love with a Tahitian prince but was prohibited from marrying him because she was a commoner.

UTUROA

Uturoa is the capital and main port of Raiatea and also is the administrative centre for the Leeward Islands. It is the second largest town in French Polynesia and although it is no metropolis it has its own electrical power station, a hospital, gendarmerie, court, Chinese stores, small hotels, three banks, boutiques, post office, pharmacy, Air Polynesie office, schools and a barber shop. There is also a plant which makes the ice used to refrigerate fish exports to Papeete and a municipal market. The market comes alive at the crack of dawn on Wednesdays, Fridays and Sundays. If you become bored or want companionship, there are always yachts moored at the wharf whose occupants are eager to trade stories and consume beer.

Around Town

The most important tourist development

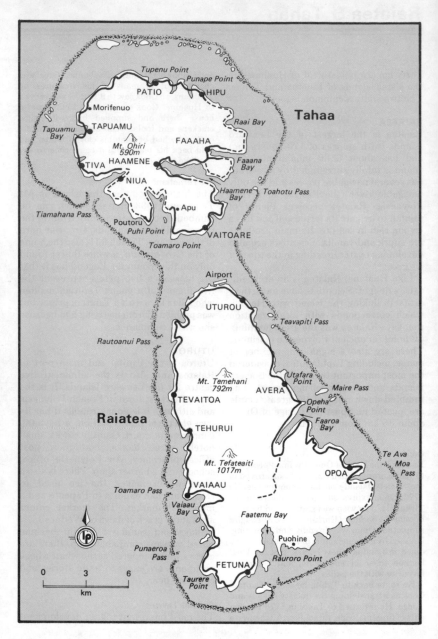

Tahaa

Tupenu Point
Punape Point
PATIO
HIPU
Morifenuo
Raai Bay
Tapuamu
TAPUAMU
Bay
FAAAHA
Mt. Ohiri
590m
HAAMENE
Faaana
TIVA
Bay
NIUA
Haamene
Bay
Toahotu Pass
Apu
Tiamahana Pass
Poutoru
Puhi Point
VAITOARE
Toamaro Point

Airport

UTUROU

Teavapiti Pass

Rautoanui Pass

Mt. Temehani
792m
Utafara
Point
AVERA
Maire Pass
TEVAITOA
Opeha
Point
TEHURUI
Faaroa
Bay

Raiatea

Mt. Tefateaiti
1017m
Te Ava
Moa
Pass
VAIAAU
OPOA
Toamaro Pass
Vaiaau
Bay
Faatemu Bay
Puohine
Punaeroa
Pass
Rauroro Point
FETUNA
Taurere
Point

0   3   6
km

Top: Singers competing during Bastille Day celebrations, also known as Tiurai (RK)
Left: Young dancer practising (RK)
Right: Dancer during Tiurai celebrations (RK)

Top: Typical church in the Tuamotus (TTB)
Left: Nuku Hiva in the Tuamotus (TTB)
Right: Huahine (JW)

on Raiatea is the Bali Hai Hotel (36 units), which is very small by most standards. The Bali Hai organises the only excursions on Raiatea, which include visits to some of the marae, trips up the Faaroa River (traditionally the departure point for the ancient Polynesians who settled Hawaii and New Zealand), canoe trips to the nearby island of Tahaa and a trek up to Mt Temehani to see the apetahi flower. Culturally, one of the most unusual aspects of Raiatea is that firewalking is still practised on the island. The Bali Hai also organises firewalking exhibitions.

Near the town is Tapioi Hill, where in 1974 a television relay station was installed. A climb to the top provides an excellent view of Raiatea and the neighbouring islands.

Scuba Diving

The lagoon offers excellent diving and the local Raiatea Spear Fishing and Scuba Diving Club provides equipment rentals, transportation and lessons for diving enthusiasts. For details contact M Patrice Philip, PO Box 272, Uturoa, Raiatea (tel 6-35-04).

Places to Stay – bottom end

Hotel Raiatea Village (tel 6-31-62) has seven seaside bungalows (with kitchenettes) and five 'garden' bungalows (with kitchenettes). The hotel is located near the Avera area (PK 11). Bicycle, canoe and car rentals are available. Tariffs for the seaside bungalows are 6000 cfp per day (one or two people), 7500 cfp for three people and 9000 cfp for four people. Garden accommodation is 5000 cfp per day (one or two people), 6500 cfp for three people and 8000 cfp for four people. Three meals a day costs 2000 cfp extra. Write PO Box 282, Uturoa.

Pensions *Pension Yolande Roopinia* (tel 6-35-28) is in Avera at PK 10. The pension has four rooms with kitchen; price includes breakfast and dinner. They have bicycles for rent. Excursions to the ancient Taput-aputea Temple and picnics on *motus* are also available.

Pension Ariane Brotherson (tel 6-33-70) requires a deposit of 3000 cfp for confirmed reservations. Send it to Ariane Brotherson, PO Box 236, Raiatea. There are two rooms, three people maximum per room. Rates are 4500 cfp per day (single) and 8000 cfp per day (double). The address is Avera, PK 8.

Located six km outside Uturoa, *Chez Sylvere Commings* (tel 6-32-96 or 6-30-92) has three rooms (each with double bed), common bathroom; cost including breakfast and dinner is 4000 cfp per day for a single and 7000 cfp per day for a double. One room is also available in Uturoa – it has two beds, private bathroom and kitchenette; cost is 2000 cfp per day for a single or a double. Bicycle and windsurfing rentals are available. The address is PO Box 190, Uturoa.

Places to Stay – top end

The newest *Bali Hai* (tel 6-13-59) is located on a lagoon five minutes from the airport very near the town of Uturoa. It offers deep-sea fishing, water skiing, bicycling and guided tours to the Faaroa River by outrigger. Prices begin at 9800 cfp for a single and 11,900 for a double.

Places to Eat

There are two local bars in Uturoa – the *Alamoana* and the *Three Stars*. The *Vairahi* is a disco. Outside of town you can try the bar at the Bali Hai. Uturoa also has several small restaurants – *Jade Garden, Au Motu, Te Orama, Chez Remi, Maraamu* and the airport snack bar.

TAHAA

Tahaa's area is 90 square km and the population numbers approximately 3500. It is not as fertile as Raiatea, doesn't get as much rainfall, is more isolated and consequently is less economically developed. Being somewhat of a backwater, it is even more tranquil and off the beaten track. With the exception of accommodation with locals, there are no places to stay. The island is surrounded by a reef with two passes and is served both by regularly scheduled inter-island boats from Papeete and local ferry boats from Raiatea. Travel time by boat from Raiatea is about 20 minutes. Agriculture is mainly in the form of subsistence farming although vanilla and copra are produced commercially. Livestock and chicken ranches are also important. Local crafts such as hand-woven hats, baskets, place mats, bedspreads, shell necklaces and wood sculpture are a cottage industry for many.

One story about the island, recently substantiated, concerns the survivors of a Chilean slave trader wrecked near the village of Tiva in 1863. Before the rescue party arrived, several of the crew members disappeared. They hid in the village, married islanders and became the ancestors of Tahaa's 'Feti Panior' – the Spanish clan. To this day, their descendants live in Tiva and are renowned for their beauty.

PATIO

The capital of Tahaa is Patio, located on the northern portion of the island. It has a gendarmerie, an infirmary, a post office (with radio telephone) and a school. Excursions to points of interest can be arranged with locals, including visits to spots where the mythical Polynesian hero – appropriately named 'Hiro' – left his mark. These landmarks consist of Hiro's bowl, file, left footprint, crest and boat. The tiny islet of Hipu off the coast of Tahaa is the home of Hiro's shark. There are some strikingly beautiful bays on the island, including Haamene and Hurepiti, which a local guide will be glad to show you.

Places to Stay

Inquire at the Maire in Patio regarding *Chez Simeon Chu*. Studio accommodation is 2500 cfp per day (single or double). You can also ask about *Chez Mata Marae*. It has two rooms and a common bathroom. Rates are 2500 cfp per day (single or double).

Getting There

Raiatea and Tahaa can be reached by inter-island steamer from Papeete. The *Temehani II* and the *Taporo IV* take about 19 hours. The *Taporo I* sails regularly from Raiatea to Bora Bora, Huahine and Maupiti.

Flights with Air Polynesie are available to Raiatea seven days a week from Papeete and flight time is 45 minutes. There are also regular flights to and from Bora Bora, Huahine, Manihi, Maupiti, Moorea and Rangiroa. See the introductory Getting Around section for more details.

Getting Around

On Raiatea, taxis are available as is Le Truck service to all the outlying districts between 5 am and 6 pm. Car rentals can be arranged with Suzanne Guirouard, tel 6-33-09 in Uturoa, from 6000-7000 cfp per day, including 10 litres of gas and insurance.

For motorcycle, scooter and bicycle rentals contact Charles Brotherson in Uturoa. Rates are about 4000 cfp per day for a motorcycle, 3000 cfp per day for a scooter and 800 cfp per day for a bicycle.

On Tahaa, contact M Petit Tetuanui in Tiva for information regarding excursions. For car rentals, find M Henri Tupaia in Poutoru.

Bora Bora

Just 16 km west of Tahaa lies Bora Bora. Dominated by two towering volcanic peaks and by locals who have learned a thing or two about capitalism, the island has been the subject of much publicity. Formerly a quiet retreat, it is now a mecca for American tourists, hotel entrepreneurs and, recently, Italian film-makers. At the moment it is slated by the Tahitian government (along with Tahiti and Moorea) for major tourist development, including a 154-room Hyatt Hotel.

Bora Bora is also a microcosm of the extremes French Polynesia has to offer. No superlatives can adequately describe the spectacular beauty of its emerald-green hills and crystalline blue lagoons. At the same time, visitors may find that locals sometimes have an understandably jaded attitude towards tourists (of whom perhaps they have seen too many). The lesson has not gone unnoticed on other islands. Residents of neighbouring Maupiti shake their heads when they speak of changes on Bora Bora and vow that the same thing will not happen on their island.

Through the years, Bora Borans have learned to cope with an ebb and flow of foreigners. During WW II, 6000 American troops were stationed on the island. The principal remnant of this occupation (aside from the Bora Borans fathered by Americans) is the airstrip. In 1977 the island was again occupied, this time by an army of Italian film-makers shooting Dino De Laurentiis' production of *Hurricane*. Again the economy boomed – local merchants turned a handsome profit and many of those hired by the movie-makers were riding new motorbikes or playing new cassette decks. When the Italians left, business as usual became the order of the day. Women returned to work in the hotels and men returned to their fishing boats. The islanders' flexibility is both admirable and a matter of survival.

American author James Michener has written a great deal about Bora Bora and in his epic *Hawaii* offers the theory that the island was a jumping-off point for Polynesian mariners who settled Hawaii. Michener's novel suggests that the reason for this migration was religious persecution.

AROUND THE ISLAND

Bora Bora is about 32 km in circumference and the best way to see it is from a bicycle seat. Bikes can be rented in many locations and some hotels lend them to visitors as part of the tariff. Depending on what form of conveyance you use, the round-the-island tour can take from 90 minutes to several hours. The tour starts from the Hotel Bora Bora and goes anti-clockwise around the island.

Martine's Creations (0.5 km)
This small boutique selling black pearls and hand-painted T-shirts is one of many boutiques and locally run crafts stands, an important cottage industry on the island.

Restaurant/Hotel Matira (1 km)
Good basic Chinese cafe serving inexpensive food. The same proprietor has very reasonably priced bungalows with kitchen facilities.

Matira Point (2 km)
Best beach on the island.

Hotel Marara (3 km)
Hotel catering to mostly French clientele. Built in 1977 by film maker Dino De Laurentiis to house his movie crew during the filming of *Hurricane* (which was a dreadful bomb).

Anua Village (8 km)
Most typically Polynesian of the villages on Bora Bora. Includes churches, a

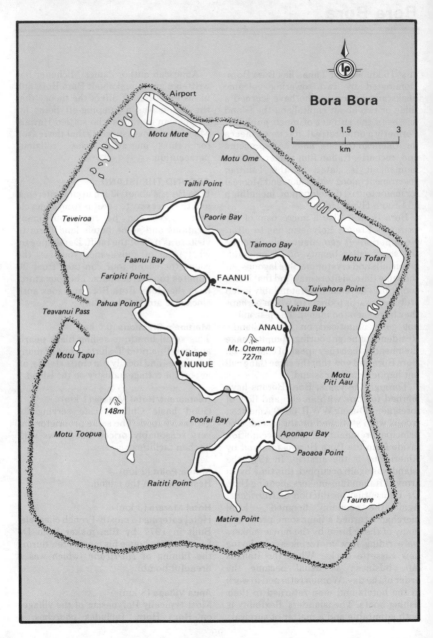

Bora Bora

N

0   1.5   3
km

Airport

Motu Mute

Motu Ome

Taihi Point

Paorie Bay

Teveiroa

Taimoo Bay

Faanui Bay

Motu Tofari

Faripiti Point

FAANUI

Pahua Point

Tuivahora Point

Teavanui Pass

Vairau Bay

ANAU

Motu Tapu

Mt. Otemanu
727m

Vaitape
NUNUE

Motu
Piti Aau

148m

Motu Toopua

Poofai Bay

Aponapu Bay

Paoaoa Point

Raititi Point

Taurere

Matira Point

school, a general store and rambling, tin-roofed homes with well-kept gardens. If a sudden thirst strikes you at this point, visit *Tutu's Bar*, a shack with a refrigerator filled with Hinano Beer. Ask around and the owner will open the bar (assuming it is unoccupied already) especially for you.

Mt Otemanu/Otemanu Cave (8.5 km)

At this juncture you are in the shadow of Mt Otemanu, highest point on the island. Near the summit but not easily accessible is the cave, formerly a burial area. On its walls, graffiti proclaims that 'Kilroy was here.' Do not attempt to climb to the cave – the ascent is steep and dangerous.

Marae Aehua-tai (11 km)

Upon reaching the summit of the island's only hill, do not speed down. The road may be rutted and ultimately unhealthy for downhill racers. Descending from the hill to the beach below is a path to Marae Aehua-tai, an ancient Polynesian temple, and one of several on Bora Bora. The next several km past the temple are virtually uninhabited, sprinkled only with a few houses and several banana groves, coconut palms and taro patches. The mosquitoes may be troublesome if you need to stop the bike to relieve yourself of Tutu's beer.

Bora Bora Bungalows/Hyatt Hotel Site (17 km)

The 'bungalows' perched on stilts on the hillside are condos, some of which are owned by Jack Nicholson and Marlon Brando. Don't look too hard, though; chances are the stars will be enjoying other tax write-offs than these. Adjacent to the bungalows is the site of a future Hyatt Hotel due for completion in 1986. The Hyatt complex will be the largest on the island.

Marae Fare-Opu (19 km)

This temple is just along the side of the road. Look for turtle petroglyphs engraved on some of the slabs. Turtles were a sacred animal to the ancient Polynesians, and were only consumed by chiefs and priests.

Faanui Bay/Village (20 km)

This is the section of the island where most of the 6000 American servicemen were stationed during WW II. Visible in the area are pilings from a dock, a concrete ramp that descends gently into the water for seaplanes, and a quonset hut nestled in the bushes along the roadside. Also visible is a massive ammunition bunker on the hillside. The Bora Bora operation was code-named 'Bobcat.'

Hikers might be interested in finding the Faanui trail, a path that traverses the island. To get there ask for the road to the garbage dump and note the old ammunition bunkers on the side. Continue past the dump on foot and you will see several old marae. As the trail continues the jungle growth becomes more dense and the trail may be a bit rough for the average hiker.

Marae Marotetini (21 km)

A five-minute walk from the road, this was the most important temple on Bora Bora and was restored in 1968 by Dr Y H Sinoto. It was used in the old days by a religious sect entertaining the local population. Near the marae are two tombs built for the Bora Bora royal family during the last century.

Stories of those who purposefully or inadvertently defile the old shrines and suffer the consequences abound in French Polynesia. Supposedly in 1973 a labourer working near Marae Marotetini discovered a rusted biscuit tin containing what were believed to be the charred remnants of the clothing of the last queen of Bora Bora. The tin was accidentally destroyed and not long afterwards (despite the efforts of modern medicine) the worker died of a mysterious malady. According to author Milas Hinshaw's account of the incident in *Bora Bora E*, after the worker's death his body 'turned black – resembling a corpse that had been consumed by fire.' Hinshaw and his son claim to have been cursed by this same marae when they picked up several human bones there and took them home as souvenirs. Not until five years later, after returning the bones to their resting place, did the author's spate of bad luck stop. Why it took him five years to figure this out, I do not know.

Faanui Power Station (21 km)
Located in the village of Faanui, this steam generator is powered by coconut husks. Several hundred metres past the station is a sturdy freight dock built by the US Seabees during the war, still used as the major freight unloading facility on Bora Bora.

Le Recife (21.5 km)
The island's only after-hours haunt. Weekends are the best.

Yacht Club (22 km)
Watering hole and accommodation.

Club Med/Trail to Big Guns (23.5 km) Near Club Med is a path leading up the hill to two Mark II coastal defence guns, each seven inches in diameter, manufactured by Bethlehem Steel. They protected Teavanu Pass directly below, the island's only access to the ocean. Ask at Club Med for directions. The Club Med scene at Bora Bora is smaller than the one on Moorea and is also one of the few night spots around the island.

Oa Oa Hotel (24 km)
This hotel has replaced the Yacht Club as the current 'in' spot. Generous American-sized drinks are served as well as Mexican food on Fridays.

Chez Rariu (24.5 km)
Newly opened restaurant with a good reputation for seafood and French cuisine.

Viatape Village (25-26 km) Bora Bora's major community. A plethora of shops and boutiques include *Magazine Roger* (a general store); *Establissements Loussan* (best selection of meat and produce); *Chin Lee* (largest market on the island) and a gas station. There are also banks, schools, a gendarmerie, the Air Polynesie bureau (located in the mayor's office), post office (which boasts a new microwave installation for international calls), a commercial centre which has a doctor/dentist office, bank, *Bora Bora Burgers* and the (argh) *Pakalola Boutique*. There are also several inexpensive pensions (see listing below).

Chez Lulu (26.5 km)
Another recommended restaurant serving seafood and pepper steak. Just past the restaurant is the weathered facade of a mansion built by De Laurentiis as a 'replica' of the governor's mansion in American Samoa for *Hurricane*.

Tatu's Museum (29 km)
The two large hulks of ships on the reef, a collection of anchors, a Mark II coastal defence gun, the carcasses of army vehicles and other objects strewn around make up what is informally known as 'Tatu's Museum.' Tatu is a large Tahitian who likes large things. He lives in the A-frame behind the collection which makes up his front yard. Tatu's aim is to convert the ships into a floating bar/museum some day. Don't hold your breath on this project.

Bloody Mary's (30 km)
A Bora Bora institution.

Moana Arts (31.5 km)
Fine shop run by famous Tahiti photographer Erwin Christian. Great selection of cards, posters and fashions.

Hotel Bora Bora (32 km)
Swankiest hotel on the island, run by Monty Brown, an American from Hawaii. It caters primarily to American guests – excellent restaurant and ritzy, spacious bungalows.

PLACES TO STAY
Bottom end

Ten minutes from the airport is *Yacht Club de Bora Bora* (tel 6-70-69) with over-the-water bungalows and five out-of-the-ordinary floating bungalows, restaurant and bar. There are facilities for yachts as well as water sports, deep-sea fishing and scuba diving. Prices are 6500 cfp per day for a single and 7800 cfp for a double. Over-the-water bungalows are 19,000 cfp per day. Write PO Box 17, Viatape, Bora Bora.

A fun place to stay is *Bloody Mary's*, located near the Hotel Bora Bora. It has five bungalows (double occupancy with kitchenettes), snorkelling, outrigger canoes and a Tahitian-style restaurant. Bloody Mary's is a well-known landmark – a sign outside the entrance lists the luminaries who have visited there (including Ringo Starr and Julio Iglesias). Rates are 5500 cfp per day for single or double. The address is Box 38, Bora Bora.

Hotel Royal Bora Bora (tel 6-71-54) in the main community of Viatape has eight bungalows with two single beds or a double bed (including bathroom) and three rooms with two single beds (common bathroom). Rates are 6000 cfp per day (including breakfast and dinner) for a single, 8000 cfp per day for a double and 13,500 per day for triple occupancy. Individual rooms (including breakfast and dinner) are 3500 cfp per day per person.

Hotel Miri-Miri has five bungalows with double beds (including individual bath-rooms), a restaurant and a bar. It is located a few minutes from the airport. A bungalow with two meals is 6200 cfp per day (single) and 11,700 cfp per day (double). Without meals, the bungalow is 4600 cfp per day per person. A 5000 cfp deposit is required for each reservation. The address is PO Box 74, Viatape.

Pensions *Chez Aime* in Viatape is a house with eight rooms and a common bathroom. Maximum capacity is 18; accommodation is quasi-dormitory-style. It's a best bet for budget travellers, but is the kind of place that has no hot water. The host, Aime, is a laid-back Tahitian who may throw in breakfast with the price of lodging. Rates start at 1200 cfp per day per person for the first night, 1000 cfp for the second and 800 cfp for the third or more.

Bungalow Are (tel 6-70-73) has one bungalow and two rooms with double beds, kitchen and bathroom. The address is Matira-Nunue. Cost is 7000 cfp per day.

Chez Celina (tel 6-70-80) has one bungalow (three people maximum), a bathroom and a restaurant on the premises. Rates are 5000 cfp per person per day. Write PO Box 21, Viatape.

Also in Viatape is *Chez Denis* (tel 6-72-08), with two double rooms and a common bathroom. Rates are 2000 cfp per day (single) and 3000 cfp per day (double). Rates with one, two or three meals a day are negotiable.

Chez Fredo (tel 6-70-31) has three rooms with two single beds (common bathroom) and three bungalows with kitchenettes and private bathrooms. For a confirmed reservation a 2000 cfp deposit is required. Rates are 1000 cfp per person per day (for rooms); the cost goes down to 900 cfp per day after one night. Bungalows range from 4000-5000 cfp for one or two people, two-day minimum. Phone or write M Alfred Doom, Viatape.

In Faanui, *Chez Jacqueline Robson* (tel 2-06-03 in Tahiti) offers one very modern bungalow (No 16) with two double rooms – four-person maximum. For one or two people the cost is 17,000 cfp per day; for three or four people it is 20,000 cfp per day. The address is Faanui on Bora Bora or PO Box 6114, Faaa, Tahiti.

Chez Louise Murfey (tel 2-06-03), also in Faanui, offers Bungalows No 18A and No 11, both with two double rooms, kitchen-ette and bathroom. No 18A goes for 10,000 cfp per day (one or two people) or 14,000 cfp for three or four people. No 11 goes for 21,000 cfp per day (one or two people) or 28,000 cfp for three or four people. Write c/o Jacqueline Robson, PO Box 6114, Faaa, Tahiti.

Located at Matira Point on the beach, *Chez Nono* (tel 6-71-38 or 6-72-16) offers two bungalows with two double rooms – one with a private bathroom, the other with a common bathroom. For reservations write or call Noel Levard. A deposit of 4000 cfp is required. A room with breakfast is 4000 cfp per day for a single and 7000 cfp per day for a double. Dinner costs 1800 cfp per person. Write PO Box 12, Bora Bora.

Chez Rosina (tel 6-70-91) has four rooms with double beds – two with private bathrooms and two with common bathrooms. Rates for one or two people are 2000 cfp per day (without meals) or, if you want breakfast and dinner, 4000 cfp per day for a single, 7000 cfp per day for two people. The address is PO Box 51, Nunue.

Situated on the tiny islet of Toopua, *Fare Toopua* (tel 8-26-12 in Tahiti) is a five-minute boat ride from Viatape and 50 metres from the beach. Accommodation is two bungalows with kitchens, bathrooms and cooking utensils – four people per bungalow. Rates are 6600 cfp per bungalow per day – three-day minimum stay. Monthly rental is negotiable. Boat rental is available. For reservations write Mme Annie Muraz (PO Box 87, Bora Bora) or call the above number. A 20% deposit is required based on the tariff for a confirmed reservation.

Camping The campground is run by the bus driver for Hotel Climate Bora Bora, Philippe Selio Vaino, and is located two km south of Anau Village. He can be easily met on the incoming boat from the airport. Cost is 300 cfp per day, which includes hot and cold running water. Reports are that the owner generously gives campers bananas, papayas and coconuts. A 500 cfp fee pays for transportation from boat to campground. There is free bus service to Viatape daily.

Middle
Located eight km from the village of Viatape near the finest beach on the island is *Hotel Matira* (tel 6-70-51). It has 28 bungalows, some with kitchenettes. There is a good, inexpensive Chinese restaurant on the premises (prices range from 900-1450 cfp and the menu includes chop suey, seafood, fish and lobster). Car, scooter and bicycle rentals are available at 6000 cfp, 4000 cfp and 800 cfp respectively for daily use. Prices begin at 6800 cfp for a single and 8000 cfp for a double. The address is PO Box 31, Viatape, Bora Bora.

Noa Noa (tel 2-96-99) – a Club Med village – is much smaller and more intimate than the Club Med on Moorea. It has a bar, restaurant, night club, excursions and all the usual Club Med activities. The Noa Noa is the 'hottest' social scene on Bora Bora with dancing every evening. It is 1½ km from Viatape and offers all water sports. There are 41 twin units. Prices are US$600 per week per person including three meals and all sports. Write PO Box 38, Nunue, Bora Bora.

Hotel Oa Oa (tel 6-70-84) is an American-owned establishment with 14 Tahitian-style *fares*, water sports activities, six yacht moorings and a white sand beach. It is considered the 'in' spot for yachties. Generous American-style drinks are served at the bar and Mexican food is dished up on Friday nights. The hotel is located on the Viatape lagoon one km from the ocean terminal. Rates are 7700 cfp for a single and 9800 cfp for a double. Pensions are available beginning at 3750 cfp per night per person. The address is Box 10, Nunue, Bora Bora.

Top end
Hotel Bora Bora (tel 8-12-06) is perhaps the finest hotel on Bora Bora, with a good reputation for service and cuisine. It is owned by the same people who own the Tahara'a; consequently the same American visitors come here as well. There are 80 bungalows (including 15 over the water), a

conference room, restaurant, two bars, a boutique, snorkelling, canoes, tennis, a white sand beach and bicycles. Car rentals are available at the hotel. Charter cruises are available with American expat Rich Postma, a veteran skipper who is savvy to the ways of French Polynesia. The Bora Bora is located six km from the main village of Viatape in Nunue, Bora Bora. Prices begin at 22,475 cfp for a single and 24,650 cfp for twin.

Hotel Marara (tel 2-60-70) was originally constructed by Italian film producer Dino De Laurentiis during a film production on the island. Located on Matira Beach, it has 64 bungalows, a restaurant, bar, boutique, all water sports activities, tennis, jeep tours, car rentals, windsurfing, deep sea fishing, a disco, bicycles, glass-bottom boat trips and cruises. The clientele is mostly European. Rates begin at 17,000 cfp for a single and 18,000 cfp for a double. Write PO Box 6, Bora Bora.

Located on the same islet as the airport, *Marina* (tel 2-95-01) offers 30 bungalows, a restaurant, bar, boutique, windsurfing, water skiing, snorkelling and a white sand beach. Prices begin at 9250 cfp for a single, 10,800 cfp for a double. The address is Motu Mute, Bora Bora.

PLACES TO EAT
In addition to the hotels, there are several good restaurants on the island. *Restaurant Muliru* near Matira Point serves basic Chinese, no frills, at 800-1500 cfp. Try *Chez Rariu* near Viatape for French and seafood, 1500-2500 cfp. *Chez Lulu* (near Viatape) has seafood and specialises in pepper steak; prices range from 1500-2000 cfp. *Bloody Mary's* by the Hotel Bora Bora offers seafood and Tahitian dishes at 1500-2000 cfp.

ENTERTAINMENT
For Bora Bora's small size, it has more hangouts than you might expect. On a

Friday evening begin the circuit by hitting the *Oa Oa* for a drink or two. More than likely there will be an informal Tahitian combo strumming away on guitars and ukeleles. On Friday nights this is the only place to get Mexican food in French Polynesia, and from all reports it is worth sampling. Next stop is the *Club Med* variety show, always good for a few chuckles. Following this it is disco time. Assuming your appetite for nightlife is insatiable (as is the case with most Tahitians), next on the agenda is *Le Recife*, the Hotel Bora Bora's only after-hours club. It is a Tahitian-style disco – crowded, noisy and full of drunks.

After the disco closes it's time to pile into the car, drive around to the other side of the island and (beer in hand) watch the sun come up. By this time you have undoubtedly worked up an appetite so like your Tahitian hosts you can breakfast on *poisson cru* (raw fish marinated in lemon juice), which is delicious and will give you the strength to carry on until the following night.

GETTING THERE

Bora Bora is accessible from Papeete via the inter-island vessels *Taporo IV* and the *Temehani II*. The island can also be reached from Raiatea with the *Taporo I*. The journey takes about a full day.

Flights are available from Tahiti seven days a week to Bora Bora and flight time is about 50 minutes. There is air service to Bora Bora from Raiatea, Huahine, Manihi, Moorea, Maupiti and Rangiroa. See the introductory Getting Around section for more details.

GETTING AROUND

All major hotels can arrange car rentals; if you are not staying at a large hotel, auto rentals can be had through Bora Bora Car Rentals, located south of Viatape; Rene Chancelades, just south of Club Med (he has scooters and bicycles too); and Alfredo Doom, who rents scooters, bicycles and autos. As mentioned before, you will find that most of the larger hotels provide bicycles for their patrons and that Bora Bora is small enough to make this type of transportation sufficient.

Maupiti is the unexploited gem of French Polynesia. It is the smallest (25 square km) and lies 37 km west of Bora Bora, the most isolated of the Leewards. In two hours, you can hike the trail that circles the island without seeing another human being. A 20-minute walk from the main village is snow-white, crescent-shaped Tercia Beach on the edge of a turquoise lagoon.

Maupitans have a disarming friendliness that matches the pristine beauty of their island. They are perhaps the most hospitable islanders in French Polynesia. There is no deluxe accommodation available on Maupiti; the visitor must either stay in a pension-style arrangement or lodge with a family. Maupitans have adopted a 'no hotel' policy to preserve the island as it is. They have had several offers to build modern hotels, which the village elders have refused – Bora Bora's hotels are just a few km away.

On Maupiti, as in many isolated communities, the residents have the curious habit of burning their lanterns all night. If you ask why, they may or may not tell you the reason is to keep the *tupapa'u* (ghosts) away. If we are to believe the inhabitants, Maupiti is a haven for every type of ghost, spirit and supernatural creature imaginable. There is even a semi-annual beach party strictly for ghosts; every so often someone from the village passes the beach while these exclusive affairs happen to be going on. Maupitans say that from the empty beach – once the site of a village – the sounds of musical instruments and laughter are quite audible.

PLACES TO STAY

Pensions Accommodation at *Chez Raioho Teroro* ('Papa Roro') in Vai'ea Village is a three-room house with one or two beds and a common bathroom; a six-room house (each room with two or three beds) with two bathrooms; and a four-room house with private bathrooms and showers. Capacity is 38 people. There is a restaurant on the premises. Rates are 3000 cfp per person per day (including three meals) or 1000 cfp without meals.

Chez Augusta Tavaearii, Vai'ea Village, is a four-room house; it has two rooms with double beds, a room with one double bed and one single, and a room with two double beds. Capacity is 10 people. Rates are 3000 cfp per person per day (including three meals), 2400 cfp per person per day (breakfast and dinner) and 1000 cfp per person per day (lunch).

Chez Anua Tinorua offers two rooms with double beds. The cost is 3000 cfp per person per day (including meals), 1000 cfp per person per day for a room only. The address is Vai'ea Village.

Located in Farauru Village, *Chez Teha Teupoohuitua* has two rooms with two double beds, three rooms with one double bed, a common bathroom and two toilets. Capacity is 14 people. Rates are 3000 cfp per person per day (including meals).

On the islet of Motu Tiapaa, *Chez Vilna Tavaerii* has two bungalows and six rooms (each with a double bed and a common bathroom). Rates, including three meals and transfers from the airport to Motu, are 4000 cfp per person per day.

Hotel Auria in Motu Hu'apiti has five bungalows, each with a double bed. There is a restaurant on the premises. The rate is 4500 cfp per person a day with three meals. Transfer to the airport is extra.

GETTING THERE

Maupiti is regularly served by the *Taporo I* from Raiatea. Flights are available twice a week from Bora Bora, Raiatea, Papeete and Huahine. Flight time is 30 minutes from Raiatea and 20 minutes from Bora Bora. See the introductory Getting Around section for more details.

The Tuamotus

The Tuamotus, also called Paumoto – 'low or dangerous archipelago' – comprise one upthrust coral island, a dozen fairly large atolls and countless small atolls and reefs. The coral island, Makatea, is one of the Pacific's three phosphate islands. The 78 islands are scattered over 15° of longitude and 10° of latitude immediately east of the Society Islands. With the exception of Makatea, the islands are extremely low with an elevation not exceeding two to three metres above sea level. The Tuamotus conform to the pattern of the coral atoll. Some are complete, unbroken circles of land, while others are a necklace of islands with intervening spaces of deep channels, shallow water or bare coral rock. Fakareva and Rangiroa are good examples of large atoll islands with navigable passes into their interior lagoons.

Apart from a cultured pearl industry established over the last 15 years on several of the islands, the economy is based on copra. Harvesting copra is tedious, back-breaking work that involves splitting ripe coconuts with a machete, drying them in the sun, plucking the meat out and drying the meat once more in an area protected from land crabs – usually in overhead racks. The atolls are divided into family parcels so that each clan has sufficient land from which to harvest a crop. Thanks to subsidies from the Tahitian government, the price of copra is kept artificially high to make certain the islanders will be able to make a worthwhile income. After the copra is harvested, it is placed in burlap bags, weighed and recorded in the Chinese shopkeeper's ledger. The shopkeeper usually acts as a middleman by giving credit at his store in exchange for the crop, which is eventually shipped to Papeete via the copra boats. As in all the islands of French Polynesia, the trading schooners here are the most important link with the outside world. When a boat arrives, the entire village flocks to watch copra being loaded and staples from the mainland being unloaded. On board there may be a store run by the supercargo, who sells staples and luxury items such as cigarettes, hard liquor, chocolate and coffee.

If you have a desert island fantasy, the Tuamotus are the place to live it out. Be prepared to live on quantities of fish, rice, corned beef, stale French bread, *ipo* (a Tuamotan dumpling) and perhaps some turtle. The actual settlements consist of little more than a church, Chinese store, pier, water tower or cistern and several rows of clapboard or fired-limestone homes with tin roofs. In the evening the major pastime is playing guitar or, for the older folks, listening to Radio Tahiti, which broadcasts news, music and messages to the outer islands. For the young people, time is spent cooking, fishing, harvesting copra and planning liaisons with girl or boy friends.

The Tuamotus have an eerie ambience not found on other high islands. You notice it several days after arriving. There is something elementally different about an atoll, something you feel but which is hard to articulate. Perhaps it is because you are forced to look inward. There are no caves to hide in, no mountains to climb, no valleys to explore and nowhere to escape. You become aware that you are on an insignificant speck of coral in the middle of an immense ocean. You feel stripped of all the familiar trappings of civilisation, with nothing to fall back on. Despite the monotonous sound of lapping waves on the coral reef, the rustle of ceaseless trade winds through palm fronds and the mercilessly brilliant sun, the primal beauty of an atoll casts an unforgettable spell.

RANGIROA

Rangiroa is the largest atoll in the Tuamotus and one of the largest atolls in the world. Located 322 km north-west of Papeete, it measures 68 km in length and 23 km in width. The atoll is so wide that it is impossible when standing on one side of the lagoon to see the opposite shore. Rangiroa's lagoon has an exceptional variety and quantity of marine life. Fish of every size and description – including sharks, manta rays, jack, surgeon fish, mullet, pompano, parrot fish, grouper, puffer fish, butterfly fish, trumpet fish and eels – live in its waters. Some of the local hotels specialise in diving, snorkelling and glass-bottom boat excursions. From the port it is possible to see local divers spear fish and then feed the unfortunate, wriggling creatures to the nearest shark. Rangiroa's major drawback is that, like Bora Bora, it is a prime example of what happens to an island inundated by tourists – the locals have sometimes become indifferent to guests.

Avatoru & Tiputa

There are two main villages on the island, Avatoru (on the same islet as the Kia Ora Hotel) and Tiputa, directly on the other side of the pass. Each village has pension-style accommodation that is one-fifth as expensive as the Kia Ora. Tiputa, the major administrative community, has a 'Maire' (town hall), post office, gendarmerie, infirmary, primary school and boarding school. You'll see many trees, stately walkways and even manicured lawns – a rarity in islands where water and soil are precious commodities. Once a prosperous community with revenues coming from the pearl-shell trade, Tiputa lost its gleam and economic life with the widespread use of plastics. In its glory, soil was actually brought in by those who could afford it.

Avatoru is located near the airport and has offices of the civil aviation and fishing departments, schools, a hospital and another post office. Many of the homes in both villages are constructed from solid, limestone-fired material much like concrete in texture and durability. Their whitewash has long since worn away, leaving ancient, weatherbeaten surfaces.

Places to Stay – bottom end

Pensions *Chez Tahurai Bennett* in Avatoru near the Kia Ora Hotel has four rooms with double beds, a common bathroom and electricity from 6 am to 10 pm. Rates are 3000 cfp a day with meals.

Accommodation at *Chez Teina & Mare Richmond* in Avatoru is three bungalows – each with a double and single bed – private bathrooms and electricity between 6 am and 10 pm. Transportation to the airport is available. Rates are 4000 cfp per person per day and include meals.

Chez Jean & Temarama Ami in Avatoru has three houses with two rooms, each with a double bed. There is a common bathroom and electricity from 6 am to 1 pm and 4 pm to 10 pm. Rates are 2500 cfp per person per day, including food.

Chez Nanua & Maire Tamaehu, also in Avatoru, offers two houses with two rooms, a house with one room, a common bathroom and electricity from 6 am to 1 pm and 6 pm to 10 pm. Rates are 2500 cfp per day, including meals.

In Tiputa Village, *Chez James & Henriette* is two km from the Maire. For reservations, a deposit for one night's stay is required. Accommodation is four bungalows, each with a double and single bed and private bathrooms. Rates are 4500 cfp per person per day (includes meals and a picnic excursion to an islet).

Chez Josephine Mauri in Tiputa is a house with three rooms, each with a double and single bed and a common bathroom. Electricity is available 6 am to 11 pm. Rates are 3000 cfp per person per day including meals.

Places to Stay – middle

Village Sans Souci (tel 2-48-33) is located an hour's boat ride from Avatoru on a tiny islet or *motu*. There

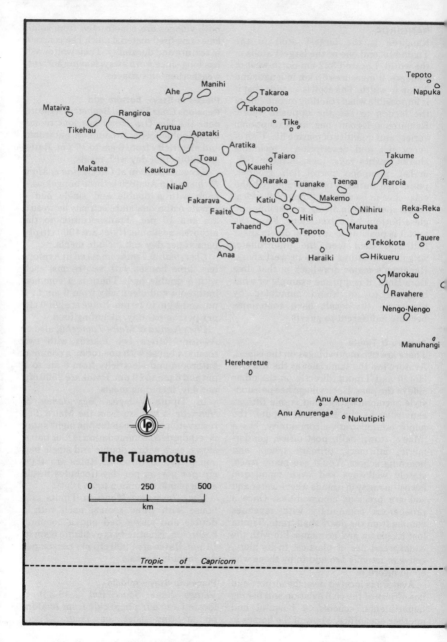

The Tuamotus

Tepoto
Napuka

Ahe
Manihi
Takaroa
Takapoto

Mataiva
Rangiroa
Tike

Tikehau
Arutua
Apataki
Aratika

Takume

Toau
Taiaro

Makatea
Kaukura
Kauehi

Niau
Raraka
Tuanake
Taenga
Raroia

Fakarava
Katiu
Makemo

Faaite
Nihiru
Reka-Reka

Tahaend
Hiti
Marutea

Motutonga
Tepoto

Anaa
Tekokota
Tauere

Haraiki
Hikueru

Marokau

Ravahere

Nengo-Nengo

Manuhangi

Hereheretue

Anu Anuraro
Anu Anurenga
Nukutipiti

0   250   500
km

Tropic   of   Capricorn

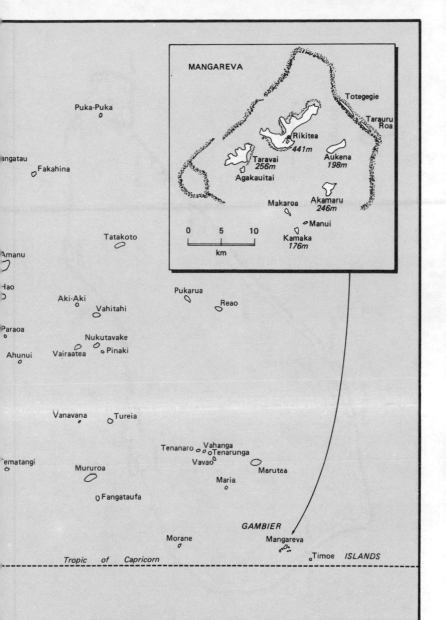

MANGAREVA

Totegegie

Tararu Roa

Rikitea
441m

Taravai
256m

Aukena
198m

Agakauitai

Makaroa

Akamaru
246m

Manui

Kamaka
176m

0   5   10

km

Puka-Puka

angatau

Fakahina

Tatakoto

Amanu

Hao

Aki-Aki

Vahitahi

Pukarua

Reao

Paraoa

Nukutavake

Ahunui

Vairaatea

Pinaki

Vanavana

Tureia

Tenanaro

Vahanga
Tenarunga

ematangi

Mururoa

Vavao

Maria

Marutea

Fangataufa

GAMBIER

Morane

Mangareva

Timoe   *ISLANDS*

Tropic   of   Capricorn

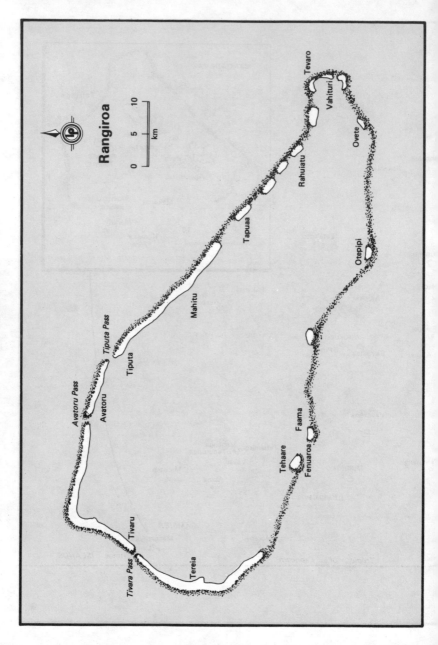

Rangiroa

are 15 bungalows, a seafood restaurant and no electricity. Visitors are provided with sheets but no maid service. The tariff includes breakfast, lunch, dinner and round trip transportation from the hotel to the airport. Activities include fishing and scuba diving. Rates are 22,850 cfp for three nights (single) and 34,700 cfp (double). A week is 38,650 cfp for a single and 66,300 cfp for a double. The address is c/o Greg and Louise Laschelle, Avatoru.

Located a km from the airport, on a beach facing the lagoon, is *La Bouteille a la Mer* (tel 1-53-34 in Rangiroa, 3-99-30 in Papeete). It has 10 double/triple bungalows, a bungalow for five people, a restaurant and a bar. Activities include snorkelling, fishing, sailing, diving, windsurfing, water skiing and excursions to islets. Rates per day are 8900 cfp (single), 15,900 cfp (double) and 21,750 cfp (triple). Write PO Box 17, Avatoru.

Places to Stay – top end
Kia Ora Village (tel 2-86-72) is the nicest hotel on this beautifully forlorn atoll. A short drive from the airport, it has 25 bungalows, five suites, a restaurant, bar and excellent facilities for diving, which is the main attraction. Complementary activities include snorkelling, windsurfing, sailing and fishing. Rates begin at 15,000 cfp for a single and 20,400 cfp for a double. Write PO Box 306, Papeete.

Getting There
Inter-island schooners to Rangiroa include the *Manava I, Manava II, Saint Corentin* and the *Aranui*. Travel time varies but may be a week or more.

There are flights seven days a week from Papeete. The flight time is 70 minutes. The island is also connected by air with Bora Bora, Huahine, Manihi, Moorea and Raiatea.

MANIHI
Although Manihi is the only other atoll in the Tuamotus with a major hotel (Kaina Village), the inhabitants are much more hospitable. The presence of the hotel and a cultured pearl industry have made the island a comparatively prosperous community. In the Tuamotus, prosperity means owning Mercury outboards, Sony tapedecks and clothing without holes. Islanders embrace their improved standard of living because they know what it is like to do without. The old outhouses built on stilts over the water's edge serve as graphic reminders of the way life was not too long ago.

Manihi's villagers take pride in their limestone and clapboard homes, which are lined along two main 'streets' of sand. Most homes have attractive front and back yards arranged with shells, shrubs and flowers. They are either fenced in or surrounded by kerbs to discourage the bands of scrawny, marauding dogs that always populate Polynesian villages. There is one main concrete dock, a flagpole and a village square where old people gossip under the shade of a huge tree.

Kaina Village
Kaina Village is a smaller-scale operation than Kia Ora and boasts bungalows constructed over the lagoon's shore that have self-contained waste treatment systems. Although the hotel is isolated from the village, it is more accessible to guests than are the villages in Rangiroa, and visitors are apt to have more contact with locals. Spearfishing is good in the lagoon, and the villagers have an easy time catching dinner in their fish trap. Kaina Village once inspired a popular song on the Tahitian hit parade called, appropriately enough, *Kaina Village in Manihi.*

Local Pearl Industry
Whatever songs the hotel may inspire, the real bread and butter comes from the island's 15-year-old cultured pearl industry. Throughout the lagoon are rows of stakes resembling barbecue spits. From these hang metal rods to which growing oysters are wired. They produce lustrous 'black pearls' with a silver sheen

unique to French Polynesia. Every year, Japanese specialists are flown into Manihi to implant tiny spheres of Mississippi River mussel shell in the black pearl oysters collected from the lagoon by local divers. After three years the oysters are harvested. Out of every 100 oysters, only seven will yield commercially usable pearls.

The hotel gives an excellent tour of the pearl facilities, located in an unobtrusive shack nearby on the village waterfront. The tour includes a boat ride in the lagoon, where a diver is sent to retrieve an oyster. The 'ripe' oyster is opened and the pearl is extracted and passed around the boat for inspection by the guests. There are no free samples; prices for a 'cheap' string of pearls start at around US$500 and go up exponentially from there. A more affordable souvenir is the 'demi-pearl,' a sort of pearl on the half-shell. It is actually a hemisphere of plastic that has been glued to the inside of a live oyster and, over the course of a year, is overlaid with mother-of-pearl. These cost about US$15 each.

Places to Stay – bottom end
Pensions *Chez Marguerite Fareea* in Turipaoa has two rooms with double beds, a common bathroom and electricity from 6 am to noon and 6 pm to 10 pm. Rates are 3500 cfp per person per day, including meals. Airport transfer is provided; please advise as to date of arrival and flight number.

Chez Estall Turipaoa also asks that for reservations you give arrival date and flight. It has two houses, three rooms, a common bathroom and electricity from 6 am to noon and 6 pm to 10 pm. Rates are 4500 cfp per person per day including meals.

Places to Stay – top end
Kaina Village (tel 2-75-53), set in a white sand beach, has 16 bungalows and two suites, a bar, a restaurant and excellent snorkelling/diving. A visit to a nearby

black pearl 'farm' and the local Paumotu village are also attractions. Prices begin at 14,500 cfp for a single and 23,100 cfp for a double. The address is PO Box 2460, Papeete.

Entertainment
Entertainment in Manihi consists of Sunday soccer games, shooting pool, a local version of bocce ball, and catching sharks off the pier. This last is done at night with a handline attached to a giant hook baited with a chunk of moray eel. When the participants land a shark, they slash its spinal cord with a machete and extract the shark's jaw for a souvenir. Near the pier is a pool filled with harmless nurse sharks with which village boys like to wrestle for the tourists' cameras.

Getting There
The inter-island vessels *Manava I* and *Manava II* sail regularly from Papeete to Manihi; check with offices for travel times. There are flights from Papeete three times a week. The flight time (including stopover in Rangiroa) is two hours and 15 minutes. Flights to Manihi are also available to and from Rangiroa, Huahine, Bora Bora, Moorea and Raiatea.

AHE
Ahe, the most popular of the Tuamotus with the yachting community, can only be reached by launch from neighbouring Manihi. Ahe does not reap the benefits of any tourist trade or commercial pearl industry; consequently it is isolated and poor. On Manihi, most residents have modern cisterns, sleep on beds and wash their dishes under a freshwater tap. On Ahe, a cistern is apt to be a rusty oil drum, the kids may sleep on a mat on the ground, and the dishes are likely to be done in the waters of the lagoon. Items that some westerners would consider rubbish – tin cans, glass bottles and plastic bags – are all used and re-used. What Ahe lacks in comfort, however, is made up in the kindness of the inhabitants. The axiom

about 'the poorer a people, the more generous,' certainly holds true on this island. There are no locked doors, and a visitor is always offered what little the family has.

Ahe's inhabitants make their living by harvesting copra and selling fish to a refrigerated storage boat that makes a regular stop on its way to Tahiti. The island was originally settled by people from Manihi and there is a friendly rivalry between the two communities. There is one small but comfortable pension for visitors.

On Ahe, you learn to appreciate life's simple pleasures. I spent a memorable evening there with some locals. Sitting outside the home of a man whose wife was expecting a baby at any moment, we sang, passed around a battered guitar and slugged away at a bottle of Algerian red wine. The expectant father disappeared inside between songs to comfort his wife. The brilliant moon that loomed over us added to the tension in the air. The baby was not born that evening, so our vigil

continued through the next night. We traded ghost stories and passed around a bottle of cheap Caribbean rum. Finally, the father announced the birth of a girl and the entire village was invited to the man's one-room shack for a fete. Inside, the single bed where the mother held the newborn child was partitioned off by a blanket. A few jackets and a spearfishing gun hung by nails tacked to the clapboard wall, and several men sat on rough-hewn chairs drinking beer by the light of a kerosene lamp. Throughout the party, three children slept soundly on floor mats in a corner of the shack.

Getting There
There is no air service to Ahe but you can take the *Manava I* or *Manava II* from Papeete or an almost daily skiff from nearby Manihi.

GETTING THERE – THE TUAMOTUS
See the introductory Getting Around section for more details of transport to these islands.

The Marquesas

Jutting vertically from the ocean floor, the emerald-green Marquesas Islands form the most spectacular and remote archipelago in French Polynesia. Situated 1250 km north-west of Tahiti, the six major islands were settled over two thousand years ago by Polynesian mariners from Samoa or Tonga. The first European to discover them was the Spanish explorer Alvaro de Mendana, who called them Las Marquesas de Mendoza in honor of his patron, Don Garcia Hurtado de Mendoza, the Viceroy of Peru. Mendana assumed he had discovered these islands en route to establishing a new Jerusalem in the Islands of Solomon.

Called by Marquesans 'Te Henua' (The Land of Men), the islands are divided into two subgroups: the windward group in the south-east comprising Hiva Oa, Tahuata, Fatu Hiva and the smaller islets of Motane, Fatu Uku and Thomasset; and the leeward group 110 km to the north-west comprising Ua Pou, Nuku Hiva and Ua Huka.

The islands, because of their proximity to the doldrums of the equator where the south-east trade winds begin to wane, have always been in a sort of backwater of the Pacific and even in this day of air travel they remain isolated. Volcanic in origin and geologically young, they rise like spires from the sea with their jagged and precipitous profiles, and they lack reefs. There are no coastal plains, and valleys are deep, trench-like and lush. The climate in the Marquesas is hotter and wetter than that of the rest of French Polynesia. Mean temperature is 28°C.

Marquesans depended more on breadfruit and food cultivated from the land than on food from the sea, which was less accessible to them because of the lack of reefs. They were a warlike lot who practised human sacrifice and, unlike their Tahitian cousins, were cannibals.

After Mendana's discovery the islands remained undisturbed for almost 200 years until Captain Cook arrived in 1774. This was the beginning of the end for Marquesan culture. After Cook's appearance, the first whalers and slave ships came, leaving behind venereal disease, tuberculosis, influenza and virtually every other malady that white civilisation had to offer. The slavers, needing labourers for guano islands and South American plantations, picked up their unfortunate victims with promises of a better life and sold them to the highest bidder. The sum of these tragic events destroyed the Marquesan people. When Cook first visited the islands, the population numbered about 50,000. Fifty years later it was down to about 5000 and fell to 1200 before it started to grow again. Today it stands at about 7000.

The first missionaries arrived on the scene in 1798 and in the following half-century different evangelistic sects zealously competed for the souls of the Marquesans. During this period of intense missionary activity the American writer Herman Melville jumped ship from a whaler and eventually wrote *Typee* based on his experiences in the Marquesas. His autobiographical account about the effects of changes made by missionaries on the indigenous population created a storm of controversy in the US and England. In 1842 the French, just beaten to New Zealand by the English, sent Admiral Dupetit-Thouars to colonise the islands and establish a naval base but found relatively little use for them. The late 19th century was a time of darkness and death for the Marquesan race, marked by periods of savagery, killings and, as Greg Denning states in his book *The Marquesas*, 'orgiastic cannibalism.' The French administration could do little more than preside over the death of a people.

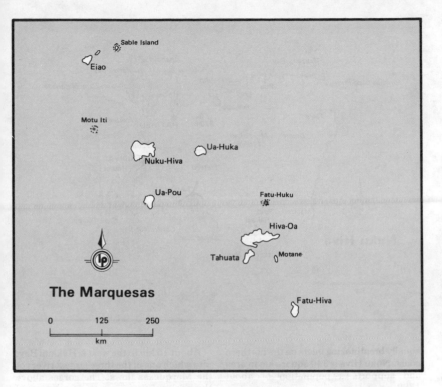

The Marquesas

```
0        125        250
|---------|----------|
         km
```

The Marquesans were most famous for their skill as tattoo artists and carvers of wood and stone. Today they still carve statues and bowls but skilled artisans are few. The remains of their temples and imposing stone tikis still stand.

Perhaps the most maddening thing about these islands is a tiny, ubiquitous creature called the 'no-no,' a nasty gnat whose bite causes an itching welt.

Economy

The islands' main product is oranges, which were exported to California, New Zealand and Australia in the 19th century. Local artisans are famous for woodcarvings and hand-crafted ukuleles.

The islands are visited often by yachts from the United States because they are the first landfall en route to Tahiti. Not many other tourists see the Marquesas because air service is limited and flights are booked up to six months in advance. The flight takes seven hours; the journey by copra boat takes seven days. For this reason, the islands are among the least physically adulterated in French Polynesia. This will undoubtedly change in the near future. Tourist authorities are already planning to expand airport facilities to accommodate jet planes.

NUKU HIVA

Nuku Hiva is the most important island in the Marquesas – it is the economic and governmental centre of the archipelago. It is also dramatically beautiful, with three major bays along the southern coast and

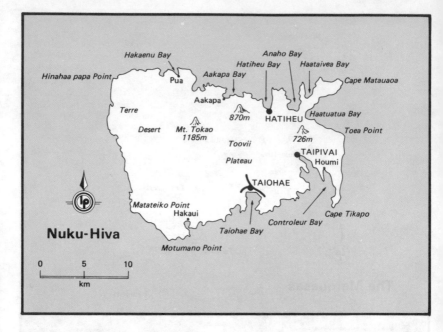

Hakaenu Bay
Anaho Bay
Hatiheu Bay
Haataivea Bay
Hinahaa papa Point
Pua
Aakapa Bay
Cape Matauaoa
Terre
Aakapa
870m
HATIHEU
Haatuatua Bay
Desert
Mt. Tokao
1185m
Toovii
726m
Toea Point
Plateau
TAIPIVAI
Houmi
TAIOHAE
Matateiko Point
Hakaui
Controleur Bay
Cape Tikapo
Taiohae Bay
Motumano Point

Nuku-Hiva

0   5   10
km

equally breathtaking inlets on the northern coast. Nuku Hiva is 340 square km in area and supports a population of about 1800.

TAIOHAE

Taiohae, the administrative centre, is located on the shores of Taiohae Bay, the central bay on the southern coast. Long visited by whalers and soldiers (both from the US and France), it has remnants of an old fort and jail built for political exiles. Aside from the usual banks, shops, post office and other government facilities the town also has the Cathedral of Notre Dame. Constructed in 1974, it is the largest church in the Marquesas and has magnificently carved sculptures adorning the interior. The Bishop's house contains a small (but still a gem) collection of Marquesan artifacts. The best view of Taiohae is from Muake, 863 metres above the bay.

About 10 km to the west is Hakauii Bay, into which one of the three largest rivers of the Marquesas flows. The gorges above the banks of the river are almost vertical and rise a thousand metres on the western side. Deep in this same valley is the Hakauii Waterfall, which cascades 350 metres down.

Tovii Plateau

The central portion of the island is dominated by the fertile Tovii Plateau. The plateau is rich in flora and fauna and the government has an agricultural station which tests potential crops and tree-planting projects.

The Coast

The west coast is high, rocky and dry; the eastern side of the island is a formidable line of sheer cliffs. Tucked away in the Taipivai Valley, just west of the coast, are many old temples called *paepae* and large tikis. It is perhaps the most beautiful valley in the Marquesas and was where Herman Melville sojourned in 1842 after deserting his whaler.

The northern bays, accessible by boat and in some cases by four-wheel-drive vehicle, are also spectacular and some have beaches. The landscape sloping down from the plateau is volcanic and almost lunar in texture. The village of Hatiheu, located on Hatiheu Bay, provides accommodation, horseback riding and boating excursions to the area.

Places to Stay

Taiohae *Hotel Moana Nui* (tel 330) is a km from the dock and has four rooms (each with one large bed) and three more rooms (each with two small beds). Bathrooms are common and the nightly cost, including breakfast, is 1500 cfp for singles, 2600 cfp for doubles. The address is c/o Robert Pelletier, PO Box 9, Taiohae.

The *Keikahahui Inn* (tel 382) is two km from the wharf and has three Polynesian-style bungalows with a view of the bay. Each bungalow has a large and small bed, hot water shower, bathroom and verandah. Including breakfast, singles are 7000 cfp, doubles 9500 cfp, triples 12,000 cfp. Activities include sunbathing on the nearby beach, diving, snorkelling, hiking, tennis, horseback riding, village tours with visits to local wood sculptors, and excursions to other bays. The inn is run by an American couple and is considered the premier resort in the Marquesas. The address is c/o Frank Corser, PO Box 21, Taiohae.

Chez Fetu (tel 366) is just 300 metres from the dock and consists of three houses, each with one room with two single beds, a room with one single, shower (with hot water), kitchen with refrigerator, stove and kitchen utensils. Rates are 1200 cfp per person per day including breakfast. The address is c/o Cyprien Peterano, PO Box 22, Taiohae.

Hatiheu *Chez Severin Katupa* is about an hours's boat ride (25 km) from the airport of Nuka Taha and is two hours by road from Taiohae. Accommodation consists of a bungalow for four people with common bath, and three other bungalows – each for double occupancy. Rates including breakfast are 1300 cfp per person per day for the larger bungalow or 2100 cfp per person per day in the smaller, double bungalows.

From Hatiheu boat excursions can be made to various bays and valleys including Aakapa, Hatiheu, Anaho, Taiohae and Pua. Fares range from 5000 cfp to 12,000 cfp. Round-trip transportation to the airport is also available for 19,000 cfp. Fishing trips cost 8000 cfp and horseback rides to ancient temples and tikis are 2000 cfp per person. The address is c/o Severin Katupa.

Getting Around

A few km inland from the northern part of the west coast is the Nuku Taha Airport – the most important in the Marquesas. To reach the main settlement of Taiohae you must take a 15-minute bus ride to the coast for 250 cfp and then catch a boat from the coast almost halfway round the island for 700 cfp. The boat ride lasts about an hour and 45 minutes.

The major points of interest on the island are accessible, but only with the proper transportation and, most of the time, with the aid of a guide.

UA HUKA

Ua Huka, around 80 square km with a population of about 500, is believed to have the oldest archaeological sites in the Marquesas and scientists postulate it was the dispersal point for settlement of the archipelago. It was never popular with early traders (because of the lack of sandalwood and protected anchorage), but today its tiny airstrip is serviced four days a week from Nuku Hiva. On Ua Huka numerous wild horses and goats run free and sometimes pilots must be wary of horses grazing near the runway.

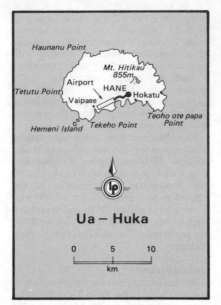

Haunanu Point

Mt. Hitikau
855m

Airport

HANE

Tetutu Point

Vaipaee

Hokatu

Teoho ote papa
Point

Hemeni Island

Tekeho Point

Ua – Huka

0   5   10

km

Main attractions are the ruins in the Hane Valley, the view from the high plateau, and excursions to Vaikivi Valley and bird islands near Invisible Bay on the southern coast. All the villages (Hane, Vaipaee and Haavai) are on the southern coast and have accommodation. The island is famous for its woodcarvers, and offshore lobster and fish are plentiful.

Places to Stay
Vaipaee Village *Chez Laura Raioha* is a house with four rooms, each with double bed, electricity, communal kitchen and toilet. Daily costs are 2500 cfp per person plus 500 cfp extra for dinner or breakfast. *Chez Joseph Lichtle* is a house with three double rooms, common bath and kitchen and electricity. Daily costs are also 2500 cfp per person. *Chez Miriama Fournier* also has three rooms available for single or double occupancy. There is a toilet, shower, electricity and common kitchen. Daily rates are 1000 cfp per person including meals.

Hane Village *Chez Vii Fournier* is a house with two rooms, each with double bed, sofa, toilet, kitchenette with refrigerator and electricity.

Haavai Village *Chez Joseph Lichtle* has three bungalows, each with double bed, private bathroom and electricity. In addition there are two houses, each with three rooms (double beds), common kitchens and bathrooms. Daily cost including meals is 2500 cfp per person. Horseback riding is available.

HIVA OA
Hiva Oa was originally named Sunday Island by Mendana when he discovered it on a Sunday in 1595. Almost three hundred years later, Robert Louis Stevenson said of the island, 'I thought it the loveliest, and by far the most ominous spot on earth.' Today it still retains this paradox of wild beauty and sombre bearing. Very little of the island's 320 square km is flat, but an airport has been laboriously constructed on a ridge above Atuona.

ATUONA
The main settlement of Atuona, the second largest town in the Marquesas, has the only safe bay on Hiva Oa, created by the flooding of a tremendous crater. Towering 1190 metres above this is Mt Temtiu, the highest point on the island. The largest building in town is the boarding school for girls, run by the sisters of St Joseph of Cluny. There are three stores, a hospital, two banks, two restaurants and a variety of accommodation possibilities with the locals.

The current population of Atuona is about 1500, only a vestige of the large population the island once had. Many homes are built on the foundations of *paepae* (temples). At one time there were many large tikis on the island but most of those that were within easy reach of the town have now been scattered to museums all over the world.

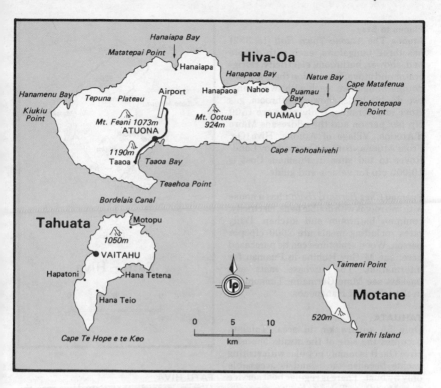

Atuona's most famous resident was Paul Gauguin, who spent the last years of his life here, and in 1903 was buried on a hill that overlooks the village. Nothing remains of his 'Maison du Jouir' (House of Pleasure), the home he built; only the well where he drew his water still exists. In Atuona, Gauguin learned from the locals how to carve wood, but found no peace on the island. He was constantly at odds with the local gendarme and priest, who looked on with displeasure at his drinking orgies with the natives. Meanwhile, the humid, sweltering climate intensified the suffering caused by venereal disease he had contracted in Paris years before. When he died, the villagers wept and the gendarme and priest sighed in relief. The only sample of his work left in Hiva Oa is a

casting of a woman's statue on his tomb. For more information on Gauguin see the introductory section on the painter.

Near Gauguin's grave is the tomb of French singer Jacques Brel, who also spent his last years on Hiva Oa and died in 1978.

Around the Coast

On the north-east coast near the village of Puamau are the largest stone sculptures in the Marquesas, considered archaeological links to the tikis on Easter Island and those of Necker Island near Hawaii. There is accommodation available in Puamau and excursions can be made to the tikis overland from the main community of Atuona.

Places to Stay

Atuona The *Atuona Town Hall* (tel 332) has three bungalows, each with double bed, shower, bathroom, electricity, refrigerator and stove. In addition there are two double bungalows, each with two rooms, two double beds, shower, bathroom, gas stove and veranda. Daily rates are 1500 cfp per person and the address is Maire d'Atuona, Village of Atuona, Hiva Oa. From Atuona visits can be made by Land-Rover to tiki sites in Puamau. Cost is 10,000 cfp for vehicle and guide.

Puamau *Chez Bernard Heitaa* has a house with two rooms with double beds, electricity, common bathroom and kitchen. Daily rates including meals are 2000 cfp per person. Wood sculptures can be purchased here; see M Guy Huhina in Puamau for information. To purchase mats and baskets see Mme Germaine Timaumoea in the village of Hanapaaoa.

TAHUATA

Only 55 square km in area, Tahuata occupies the side of the straits opposite Hiva Oa. It is mainly popular with visiting yachts because the island is accessible only by boat. There is regular boat service from Hiva Oa to Tahuata but it is generally best to notify the town hall in Tahuata 24 hours in advance to schedule a vessel. The trip takes about an hour and costs about 9000 cfp.

A small church, store and handful of dwellings are all that make up the main village of Vaitahu and serve the 550 inhabitants. There are archaeological sites here and petroglyphs in the Hanatahua Valley, which can be reached by the *Tamanu*, a boat that sails from Vaitahu.

Places to Stay

Tahuata *Chez Naani Barsinas* is a house with three rooms, each with two small beds. Daily cost including meals is 2500 cfp per person.

Fatu – Hiva

FATU HIVA

History records that Fatu Hiva was the first island to be discovered by Europeans in 1595. That encounter ended in bloodshed. Although lacking good anchorages the island was popular with whalers in the mid-19th century because it was well away from the authorities' eye and visitors could raise hell without interference.

The 80-square-km island was famous for its tattoo artists and a man might have his body tattooed completely by the time he died. Unfortunately this great art went with him to the grave. Today Fatu Hiva is the only island in the Marquesas where tapa cloth, produced from the bark of mulberry or breadfruit trees, is regularly made. Local artisans also carve wooden tikis and manufacture *monoi*, a perfumed coconut oil with fragrances derived from tiare blossoms and sandalwood.

There are two principal valleys – Hanavave and Omoa – on the western coast and each have several *paepae*. Hanavave Village, located on the Bay of Virgins, is particularly lovely. Nature has blessed Fatu Hiva with more rain than any other island in the Marquesas, giving it a land and seascape that a Tahitian described to me as 'shockingly beautiful.' The population of the island is about 400.

Other activities on the island include horseback riding and wild pig hunting. Contact the Maire (Town Hall) for further information.

Places to Stay

Omoa Village *Chez Joseph Tetuanui* is a house with two rooms and accommodation at 2000 cfp per person per day with meals. The story is exactly the same at *Chez Kehu Kamia* and *Chez Francois Peters*.

Chez Jean Bouyer has only one room

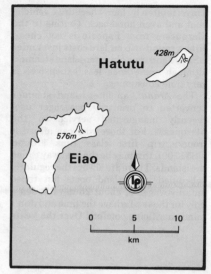

and the cost is 3000 cfp per person per day.

Hanavave Village *Chez Veronica Kamia* is a house with two rooms at the standard cost of 2000 cfp per person per day with meals. *Chez Jacques Tevenino* has just one room at a cost of 1500 cfp per person per day. Nearby are orange, grapefruit and banana trees and coffee plants. Tapa cloth and sandalwood oil processing can be observed by visitors.

Getting Around

The island is accessible by regular boat service from Hiva Oa, but there is no airstrip. The 3½ hour boat trip costs 2500 cfp per person. Travel from Omoa to Hanavave village is 300 cfp. A complete tour of the island via boat costs 10,000 cfp.

GETTING THERE – THE MARQUESAS

Visitors to these islands need to be independent travellers, patient (as in all the islands) and able to rough it a bit.

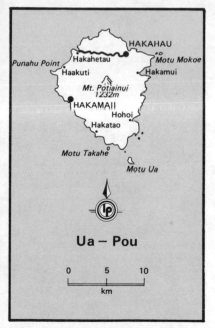

Travel is often by four-wheel-drive vehicle, boat and even horseback. Getting to the Marquesas from Papeete is not cheap either; round-trip air fare costs just under US$500 and travel by inter-island steamer, although sometimes less expensive, is very time consuming.

The *Aranui*, an inter-island steamer converted to primarily passenger use, recently inaugurated service to the Marquesas. For those who can afford it (round trip first class runs around US$1700), this may be the best way to see the islands. There are always the regularly scheduled inter-island boats but these entail voyages of about 25 days at sea – only for those who have the time and don't mind sacrificing comfort. Over the years

the most consistent visitors to the Marquesas have been American yachts which often make the Marquesas part of their itinerary because the islands are the first landfall en route to Tahiti from the west coast of the United States.

Aside from inter-island vessels such as the *Taporo V*, the *Tamarii Tuamotu* and the newly refitted *Aranui*, Air Polynesie has a regularly scheduled service two days a week from Papeete to Nuku Hiva for a fare of 39,000 cfp. From Nuku Hiva, which is in effect a hub for the other islands in the archipelago, there are flights to Hiva Oa, Ua Huka and Ua Pou. Air fares within the Marquesas range from 4705 to 8205 cfp. The other islands are only accessible by boat.

The Australs & The Gambiers

These archipelagos are the outermost and least-visited islands in French Polynesia. Lying near the Tropic of Capricorn, they are also the most temperate.

AUSTRAL ISLANDS

The Austral Islands lie about 600 km south of Tahiti and consist of five high islands (Tubuai, Rimatara, Rurutu, Raivavae and Rapa) and two atolls (Hull and Bass). The islands are of volcanic origin, not very high (100-200 metres) except for Rapa, whose highest point is 1460 metres. Rapa, the farthest south, is sometimes called Rapa Iti (Little Rapa) to differentiate it from Rapa Nui, the Polynesian name for Easter Island. Tubuai (accessible by air) is the administrative centre of the Australs and offers accommodation with local families. Rurutu (also accessible by air) has the only modern hotel in the entire region.

TUBUAI

Tubuai, largest of the Austral Islands, is windswept and has a hauntingly desolate beauty. In 1789 it was the first settlement of the *HMS Bounty*'s mutinous crew, who called their outpost Fort George. After six months of considerable bloodshed between the natives and mutineers, the Englishmen decided to leave and eventually settled on Pitcairn Island. All that remains of Fort George today is a rectangular ditch where the walls of the stockade used to be.

Since the *Bounty* episode, Tubuai has had a predilection for attracting expatriots. The best known on the island is Noel Illari,

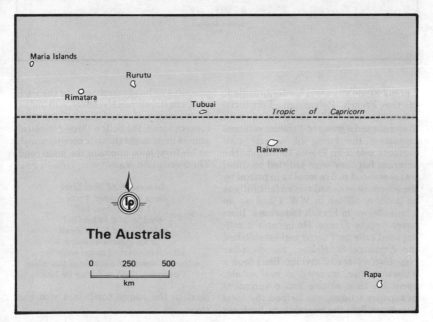

Maria Islands

Rurutu

Rimatara

Tubuai

Tropic of Capricorn

Raivavae

The Australs

0   250   500
km

Rapa

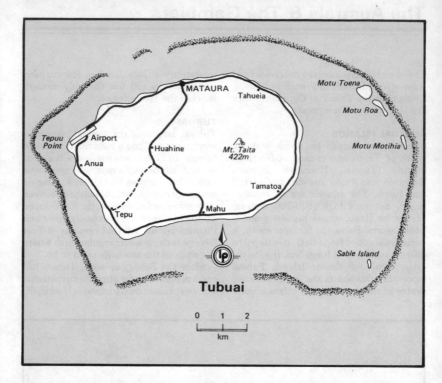

Tubuai

0   1   2
km

a proud Frenchman and former president of the French Polynesian Territorial Assembly. In 1947, Illari sided with Pouvanaa and a group of Tahitian veterans protesting the hiring of several civil servants sent from France to fill jobs the veterans felt they were entitled to. Illari was sentenced to five months in prison by the government he had served faithfully as an artillery officer in WW I and as an administrator in French Indochina. Illari never forgave France. He became a self-imposed exile on Tubuai and established the *Ermitage St Helene*, named after Napoleon's place of asylum. Illari took a Tubuaian wife, invested in real estate, spent his time writing anti-government newspaper articles, and helped the local population fight the monopolistic business practices of local merchants. In the early 1970s he developed lip cancer, and feeling he was close to death, decided to construct his own tomb. He built a three-metre-tall granite monument that sits conspicuously on his front lawn opposite the main road. The inscription reads:

In memory of Noel Illari
Born in Rennese, France
11 September, 1897
died faithful to his God
to family and to his ideals
to his grateful country
after long years of moral suffering
within isolation and solitude at this place
Passersby, think and pray for him.

Next to the empty tomb is a sign that says:

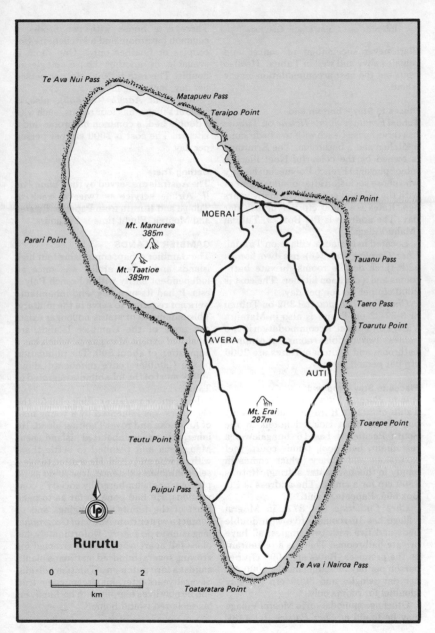

Te Ava Nui Pass

Matapueu Pass

Teraipo Point

Parari Point

Arei Point

MOERAI

Mt. Manureva
385m

Mt. Taatioe
389m

Tauanu Pass

Taero Pass

Toarutu Point

AVERA

AUTI

Mt. Erai
287m

Toarepe Point

Teutu Point

Puipui Pass

Te Ava i Nairoa Pass

Rurutu

0   1   2
km

Toataratara Point

Interdite aux Chien et aux Gaullists

Illari never succumbed to cancer and remains alive and well in Tubuai. He also rents out the best accommodation on the island.

Places to Stay – bottom end

Tubuai *Ermitage Sainte Helene* on Tubuai has three houses, each with two bedrooms, a kitchen and a bathroom. The Ermitage is owned by the colourful Noel Illari, a minor player in French Polynesian history who chose seclusion after disillusionment with the colonial government many years ago. Rates are 2000 cfp per person per day. The address is PO Box 79, Tubuai (Mahu Village).

Located in Mataura Village on Tubuai, *Chez Caroline* (tel 346) has two homes with three double rooms, private bathrooms and a common kitchen. The cost is 2000 cfp per person per day.

Chez Taro Tanepau (tel 382 on Tubuai or 3-87-32 on Tahiti) is also in Mataura Village on Tubuai. Accommodation is two homes, two double rooms, a common bathroom and a kitchen. Rates are 2000 cfp per person per day.

Places to Stay – top end

Rurutu *Rurutu Village* (tel 2-93-85 on Tahiti or 392 on Rurutu) is undoubtedly one of the most isolated hotels in the South Pacific. It has 16 bungalows, a restaurant, bar, pool, tennis court, reef excursions and library (which comes in handy in this backwater setting). Rate is 7500 cfp for a single. The address is PO Box 605, Papeete, Tahiti.

Chez Catherine (tel 377) in Moerai Village has 10 rooms – five with double beds and five with two singles; all have private bathrooms. There is a restaurant on the premises. Rates are 5000 cfp per person per day including meals, 2000 cfp per day (single) and 3000 cfp per day (double) for rooms only.

Other accommodation in Moerai Village may be found at *Chez Patrice* (tel 443).

There is a house with two rooms, a common bathroom and a kitchenette (for couples or families only). One room is available in another house, single or double. The rate is 2000 cfp per person per day, including meals.

Chez Atai Aapae (tel 455), also in Moerai Village, has four rooms, each with a double bed, a common bathroom and a kitchen. The cost is 1000 cfp per person per day.

Getting There

The Australs are served by the *Tuhaa Pae II*. Airline service is twice a week to Tubuai and Rurutu from Papeete, Raiatea and Moorea. Flight time is 2½ hours.

GAMBIER ISLANDS

The Gambier group, comprising four high islands and a few atolls, was once an independent entity within French Polynesia. It had its own flag, and inhabitants were not required to serve in the military. This independent status no longer exists and none of the Gambier Islands are inhabited except Mangareva, which has a population of about 500. The population of the Gambiers once numbered about 5000 – most of the inhabitants migrated to Tahiti.

In recent years, an exciting plan for the Gambiers was fomented by a young man of American and royal Tahitian blood. He inherited an uninhabited island near Mangareva and planned to settle there with his wife and child. He wanted to live a self-contained existence, free to do as he pleased, unencumbered by society's conventions. He had gone so far as to pack most of the family's belongings and to contact a writer from *National Geographic* magazine to do a story. Unfortunately, his plans fell apart when he was arrested for growing several hundred marijuana plants amidst a taro patch on a Tahitian hillside. Several years later, his dream came true and he now lives happily with his family on his secluded island home.

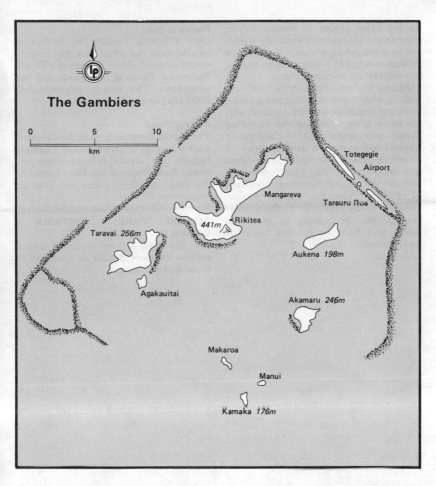

MANGAREVA

The coming of the missionaries to the Gambier Islands was anticipated in a vision by the prophetess Taopere. In 1883, the Picpus fathers of France settled on the chief island, Mangareva, and by 1836 the entire archipelago had been converted to Catholicism. Under the tyrannical leadership of Father Laval, a Belgian priest, the converts built on Mangareva the largest cathedral in French Polynesia, using fired limestone and mother-of-pearl for its interior. The strange saga of this fanatical missionary inspired one of Michener's stories in *Return to Paradise*. Although the cathedral is in need of repair, it is still in use and open to visitors. Across the path from the church is the 140-year-old rectory, occupied by the parish priest. Two km down the road is a tumble-down abbey surrounded by a well-tended vegetable garden. The garden is farmed by an industrious Mangarevan under the supervision of the priest, who sells the produce to islanders and to residents of the nearby nuclear testing site on Muroroa.

Mangareva's main industry is jewellery-making, which involves cutting and grinding items out of mother-of-pearl. Aesthetically, the island is very pleasing with its rolling brown hills reminiscent of California's coastal mountains. It is the home of French Polynesia's former vice president and venerated politico Francis Sanford, and also the home of the current president of French Polynesia, Gaston Flosse. Because of its proximity to the nuclear testing site, permission to travel to Mangareva must be secured from the government.

Places to Stay
Chez Francois Labbeyi in Rikitea is located near the wharf. For reservations write Francois Labbeyi, Mangareva, French Polynesia. There is one house and two bungalows. The rate is approximately 2000 cfp per person per day.

Getting There
The *Taporo II* regularly visits the Gambiers after a lengthy itinerary in the Tuamotu Islands. Air service is once every two weeks from Papeete via Hao. Including the stop, the flight takes just over six hours.

GETTING THERE – AUSTRALS & GAMBIERS
See the introductory Getting Around section for more details on transport to these archipelagos.

Glossary

Aito ironwood.
Archipelago group or chain of islands.
Ari'i high chiefs, the nobility of pre-European Tahitian society.
Arioi travelling minstrels and entertainers of pre-European time, making up a religious society.
Atoll low-lying island, built up from successive deposits of coral. The classic atoll is ring-shaped, enclosing a shallow lagoon.
Atua god.

Bark cloth see Tapa.
Barrier reef an offshore reef sheltering a coast or an island from the open sea but separated from the land mass by a lagoon or expanse of sea. See 'fringing reef.'
Breadfruit staple food of the South Pacific, sought after by the *Bounty* expedition to transplant in the West Indies.

Coral members of the animal group known as *coelenterates* which also include jellyfish and anemones. Corals live together in colonies and can produce a fibrous or calcified skeleton. As they die new colonies form upon the skeletons of the old and eventually a reef can be built up. Coral requires clear, warm water of an ideal depth in order to flourish.
Cyclone a powerful tropical storm which rotates around a central low pressure 'eye.' In the Caribbean a cyclone is known as a hurricane; in the Pacific it is known as a typhoon.

Embayed a coastline created by land subsidence when flooded valleys become bays.
Emergence geological activity which raises a land mass above the ocean surface to become an island.

Fare tupap'u 'ghost house,' where dead bodies were laid in pre-European Tahitian funeral ceremonies.
Fringing reef a reef found around the shore of an island or along a coast which does not contain a lagoon – see 'barrier reef.'

High island islands either volcanic in origin or the result of an upheaval from the ocean floor.

Kava beverage derived from the root of the pepper plant *piper methysticum*.

Lagoon an area of water enclosed by a reef.
Lee downwind side; to be in the lee of something is to be sheltered by it.
Leeward the side of an island sheltered from the prevailing winds – see 'windward.'
Le Truck local form of public transport; hybrid bus or jitney.

Makatea 'middle island,' atoll islands raised up by some geological disturbance.
Mana sacred essence, prestige, power.
Manahune the common people of pre-European Tahitian society.
Manava soul of a god.
Marae ancient Polynesian open temple.
Maru'ura feathered girdle, highest symbol of real and spiritual power.
Melanesian people of the far west of the Pacific characterised by their dark skins. They include the people of Papua New Guinea, the Solomons, Vanuatu, New Caledonia and Fiji.
Micronesian peoples of the north-west Pacific, believed to be of Malay-Polynesian origin. They include the people of Guam, the Marianas, the Federated States of Micronesia, the Marshalls, the northern Palau Islands and the islands of the Gilbert-Phoenix-Northern Line Islands region.

Noa non-sacred.

Ora life.
'Oro god of war and son of Ta'aroa, red feathers were his special symbol.
Oromatua ghosts.

Pahi traditional fighting canoe with raised platform above the twin hull on which the warriors would stand.
Pareu men or woman's sarong-like, wrap-around skirt.
Pirogue traditional outrigger canoe.
Pohe death.
Polynesian people who colonised the central and southern Pacific islands – including Hawaii, Tahiti, the Cook Islands and New Zealand – through great sea voyages.

Ra'atira the 'middle class' of pre-European Tahitian society.

Reef structure formed by the skeletons of coral colonies, grown over by successive generations which include the most recent, living group.

Ro'o important pre-European Tahitian god.

Seamount a volcanic mountain that does actually rise above the surface of the sea.

Seaward side of an island facing the open sea, in contrast to a side facing a sheltered lagoon.

Sennit woven coconut fibre string.

Ta'aroa important pre-European Tahitian god.

Tahu'a craftsman priest.

Tamanu ebony-like wood.

Tamure modern, hip-shaking version of a traditional dance.

Tane important pre-European Tahitian god; also a word for 'man.'

Tapa bark-cloth, the everyday clothing in pre-European Tahiti. Made by beating the inner bark of mulberry or breadfruit trees.

Tapu taboo; the English word is derived from this Tahitian word.

Taro staple root vegetable.

Tatau traditional tattoos, from which the English word is derived. Both males and females were tattooed, particularly on the buttocks. Joseph Banks was one of the members of Cook's party who came back with a tattoo.

Ti'i (or tiki) human-like wood icon, generally representing family ancestors. Particularly found on traditional canoes.

Tiputa bark-cloth poncho.

To'o symbols of Tahitian gods.

Tu important pre-European Tahitian god.

Tupap'u ghost or spirit; may be benevolent or malevolent.

Vahine woman.

Windward the side of an island facing the prevailing winds – see 'leeward.'

Index

133